PERCEPTION

THE BASICS

This book combines approaches from philosophy, psychology, and neuroscience in the study of perception. In addition to appealing to readers from all three of these disciplines, *Perception: The Basics* is a perfect introduction for students and general readers. Its interdisciplinary coverage of all aspects of perception does not require familiarity with either abstract philosophical concepts or neuroscientific knowledge.

Besides addressing the classic questions of how perception works, the book highlights the intricate connections between perception and action as well as perception that is not triggered by sensory input, like mental imagery, dreaming, and hallucination. Further, the book balances out an overemphasis on vision in the literature by giving almost equal coverage to all the sense modalities (although some examples are easier to present in visual form).

Questions that are discussed in detail include:

- What is the function of perception?
- Is perception an unbiased way of learning about the world?
- What is the difference between the different sense modalities, like seeing, hearing, smelling, etc.?
- What is the connection between perception and action?
- What is the relation between perception, mental imagery, dreaming, and hallucination?

With helpful chapter summaries and a comprehensive final bibliography, *Perception: The Basics* is sure to be the first-stop for anyone trying to better understand this important area of interdisciplinary research.

Bence Nanay is Professor of Philosophical Psychology and BOF research professor at the University of Antwerp. He published four monographs with Oxford University Press (*Between Perception and Action*, 2013; *Aesthetics as Philosophy of Perception*, 2016; *Aesthetics: A Very Short Introduction*, 2019; and *Mental Imagery: Philosophy, Psychology, Neuroscience*, 2023) with three more under contract. He is the director of the European Network for Sensory Research.

THE BASICS SERIES

The Basics is a highly successful series of accessible guidebooks which provide an overview of the fundamental principles of a subject area in a jargon-free and undaunting format.

Intended for students approaching a subject for the first time, the books both introduce the essentials of a subject and provide an ideal springboard for further study. With over 50 titles spanning subjects from artificial intelligence (AI) to women's studies, *The Basics* are an ideal starting point for students seeking to understand a subject area.

Each text comes with recommendations for further study and gradually introduces the complexities and nuances within a subject.

For a full list of titles in this series, please visit www.routledge.com/The-Basics/book-series/B

PERCEPTION

THE BASICS

Bence Nanay

Routledge
Taylor & Francis Group

NEW YORK AND LONDON

Designed cover image: Armand Khoury / Unsplash

First published 2024
by Routledge
605 Third Avenue, New York, NY 10158

and by Routledge
4 Park Square, Milton Park, Abingdon, Oxon, OX14 4RN

Routledge is an imprint of the Taylor & Francis Group, an informa business

© 2024 Taylor & Francis

Library of Congress Cataloging-in-Publication Data
A catalog record for this title has been requested

ISBN: 978-1-032-63952-9 (hbk)
ISBN: 978-1-032-63954-3 (pbk)
ISBN: 978-1-032-63953-6 (ebk)

DOI: 10.4324/9781032639536

Typeset in Bembo
by codeMantra

CONTENTS

FIGURES

PREFACE

The aim of this book is to give an interdisciplinary introduction to the study of perception. It combines philosophical, psychological, and neuroscientific approaches to the topic and should, as a result, appeal to readership from all these disciplines (as well as the general readership).

Besides the classic questions about how perception works, special emphasis is given to the intricate connections between perception and action and to perception that is not triggered by sensory input (a category that encompasses mental imagery, dreaming and hallucination). Further, too much of the (philosophical, psychological, and neuroscientific) discussion about perception has focused on vision. This book aims to correct this imbalance and give equal (or almost equal) amount of space to all the sense modalities (although some of the examples are easier to present in visual form).

There have been many introductory textbooks on vision science or perceptual psychology, which tend to get extremely technical very quickly. And there are some introductory philosophical texts, which tend to be of no interest outside of a very specific tradition of analytic philosophy. My aim was to write a book that covers all aspects of perception in an interdisciplinary manner and in a way that does not require any previous knowledge of either abstract philosophical concepts or detailed neuroscientific knowledge.

I am grateful for comments on the manuscript by Luc Faucher, Anand Vaidya, Rebecca Rowson, Ben Henke, Julian Bacharach, Andrea Blomkvist, Andrea Rivadulla Duro, Jeremy Pober, Kris Goffin, Francesco Marchi, Stephen Gadsby, Adam Bradley, Amanda Evans, Oli Odoffin, Francesca Secco, Kyle Landrum, Kael McCormack-Skewes, Alex Kerr, as well as by Stephen Biggs, who wrote a very detailed and helpful review for the press. Thanks to Adriana Alcaraz Sanchez for supplying the index. Special thanks to Andrew Beck at Routledge for approaching me with the idea of this book, and Marc Stratton, also at Routledge, for overseeing the production. The work on this book was supported by the ERC Consolidator grant [726251], the FWF-FWO grant [G0E0218N], the FNS-FWO grant [G025222N], and the FWO research grant [G0C7416N].

WHAT IS PERCEPTION?

1.1 WINDOW TO THE WORLD

Perception is our primary contact with the world. Whatever we know, we know directly or indirectly by means of perception. And the vast majority of our actions rely on perceptual guidance. The mind begins and, to be a bit dramatic, ends with perception.

When we are trying to explain how the mind works, it is a good idea to start with understanding perception. First of all, the most developed and sophisticated set of neuroscientific findings about the brain concern our perceptual processes. We understand the neural mechanisms that underpin our perceptual processes much more thoroughly than any other part of the brain. This makes perception a prime candidate for combining information from a number of disciplines in the service of understanding the mind – the endeavor often labelled 'cognitive science.' If there is a huge amount of good neuroscientific and psychological research about perception and comparatively less extensive research about other mental processes, then perception would be a good place to start such an interdisciplinary enterprise.

Further, perception is a mental process that we share with animals. The human mind is, on the face of it, very different from animal

DOI: 10.4324/9781032639536-1

minds. We seem to devote most of our mental energy to reading and writing books, conversing with friends, watching films about secret agents, playing video games, driving cars, mixing cocktails, solving sudoku puzzles, going to museums, and so on. Animals, even the smartest of them, don't do any of these.

Nonetheless, the human mind is also remarkably similar to animal minds. And much of this similarity comes from the similarity in perceptual processes. Humans see objects, as do bees. Humans hear sounds, as do dolphins. The exact mechanism that bees use to see objects may be different from the one humans use, but both count as seeing. And in some sense, it is not true that we devote most of our mental energy to all those complicated activities that I outlined in the previous paragraph. Each and every one of these activities presupposes some kind of perceptual process. So really we devote much of our mental energy to perceiving. And perceiving is something animals also do.

To put this in very abstract terms, there are two general approaches to understanding the mind. One way of doing so is to start with the human mind and its uniquely human features. The human mind has a number of fancy features, most of all language. And also abstract reasoning, rational decision-making, and so on. These are fascinating mental capacities, and it is tempting to start by trying to understand them.

But here is another way of thinking about the mind. The human mind is not that different from the minds of other vertebrates. In any case, it has evolved from animal minds, so in order to understand the exquisite complexity of the human mind, we should start with understanding something simpler: the way the animal mind represents. Once we have fully understood that, we can then, and only then, address the uniquely human fancy features, like language.

The way animals (at least vertebrates) perceive is very similar to the way we perceive. And the way animals (again, at least vertebrates) attend or exercise their mental imagery is also very similar to the way we do. So the default for understanding how the human mind represents is not to start with the uniquely human features, but with mental processes humans and other animals share, like perception, attention, or mental imagery. Once we have fully understood how these work, how they interact with each other, and how they lead to action, then and only then can we begin to address the fancy gloss on top of this fundamental representational machinery, which is uniquely human.

I once described the uniquely human features of the human mind, like language, abstract thought, and rational reasoning, as the icing on the cake (Nanay 2013): when we try to understand the cake, we should not start with the examination of the icing, we should begin with the cake itself. Understanding the icing is a nice extra perk. But if you make inferences about the cake itself from what you know about the icing, you'll get it all wrong.

How should we then try to explain perception? In this book, I argue that we should throw everything we have at this task. Psychology has been studying perception for more than a century. Neuroscience has made significant progress in the last couple of decades. And philosophers have been thinking about perception for millennia. But all these approaches use very different methods and tackle very different questions. Combining them is not easy. But it's not a new idea either.

In what is known as the interdisciplinary endeavor of cognitive science, different disciplines would interact with each other in the service of the common aim of understanding how the mind works. In an ideal case, different disciplines can learn from each other. Neuroscientists would borrow concepts from psychology and vice versa. Psychological theories, like all scientific theories, should change in response to emerging evidence, not just in psychology but also in the neighboring disciplines. And with the advent of extremely sophisticated neuroscientific methods, there has been more and more such evidence. So one important imperative for psychological theories is that they should be revised in the light of emerging neuroscientific evidence.

What role does philosophy have in all this? Can philosophy help us to understand the mind at all? Why should we pay attention to philosophers of mind at all if we have other disciplines (psychology, neuroscience), which study the very same phenomena, but with the help of hard data?

We have seen that the interaction between psychology and neuroscience is of great importance for the purpose of having as accurate a picture of how the mind works as possible. But who is supposed to integrate the most recent findings of psychology and neuroscience?

Neuroscientists are busy doing experiments and keeping up with the latest results in their field. And psychologists are busy doing the same thing in their own field. But philosophers don't have to spend their time with the daily running of labs and with ethics clearance forms. They have time to find bridges between the two disciplines.

Philosophers won't do psychology better than psychologists and they won't do neuroscience better than neuroscientists. And it is very unclear what distinctive (a priori, armchair) method they master that would add to the empirical study of the mind. But this doesn't mean that philosophy of mind is useless. One thing philosophers of mind can do and can do very well is to bring together results in different scientific disciplines and by comparing them give insights that would be valuable for each scientific discipline. So in some sense, philosophy can be the glue that holds together the diverse interdisciplinary endeavor of understanding the mind.

And the same goes for understanding perception. This book combines neuroscience, psychology, and philosophy to answer questions about perception and its role in the mental economy and in our life. Depending on the specific subject matter, the emphasis will shift between these three disciplines and approaches. But the aim throughout is to combine all possible means of enquiry. And I do this in a way that would not prioritize any one of these disciplines and also not assume any prior knowledge of any of them.

1.2 THE PROCESSING OF SENSORY INPUT

The window metaphor I started the book with is, in many ways, extremely misleading. It makes one think that our perceptual apparatus is as simple as a clear transparent glass pane. It is not. The task of perception is intricately complex and, as a result, the workings of our perceptual apparatus are equally complex.

To demonstrate just how intricately complex the task of perception is, take one of the most important sense modalities, hearing. The input of our auditory system is the movement of our eardrums. And auditory perception is supposed to decode objects in the world on the basis of this input. To give an analogy (Bregman 1990, pp. 5–6), imagine a large lake with ships and boats on it. I don't see the lake or the ships, nor do I hear them. But I can dig two narrow canals on the shore that are connected to the lake and tie a piece of cloth at the end of both canals. I can now observe the ways in which the two pieces of cloth are moved by the waves that come from the lake. That is all the input I have. And from this, I need to figure out where the ships are, which direction they are moving, which ones are bigger and when a seagull takes off from the lake.

This scenario is the almost exact mirror image of the seemingly impossible task the auditory system performs with ease. On the basis of just the movements of the eardrums, the auditory system computes the location and speed of a number of objects out there in the world (see also Section 2.2). This is an extremely complicated task.

While audition is an extreme case, the other sense modalities do not have a much easier job either. One might think that at least vision presents a more straightforward task. After all, the window to the world metaphor is implicitly about vision: we see the world through the window (don't smell, touch or taste it). But the task visual perception faces is also extremely complex. The retinal image is two-dimensional. It is the two-dimensional projection of the three-dimensional world. But there are infinitely many three-dimensional scenes that could project on the retina as one single two-dimensional image. For example, a sphere, a cone, and a cylinder would all project to the retina as a circle when seen from a certain angle – and many more three-dimensional shapes do so. Visual perception needs to figure out which of these infinitely many three-dimensional scenes is the one that is projected on the retina as this specific two-dimensional image.

In short, the sensory input our sense organs receive is pretty thin. And the task of perception is to nonetheless come up with the most likely scenario of how the world is – in spite of the scarce information carried by the input. This amounts to enriching the poor input. This enrichment comes from two sources. One is supplied by evolution. The way 3D vision manages to construct a three-dimensional model on the basis of two-dimensional input (or, rather, two pieces of two-dimensional input supplied by the two eyes) is a capacity we are all born with – it is the result of natural selection. And the same goes for the complex apparatus of auditory perception.

But not all enrichment is fixed by evolution. Some is learned in our lifetime. Natural selection has given us 3D vision, but it has given us no clue about what to do when two spotlights next to each other are approaching us. But our exposure to cars at night has taught our perceptual system to model these two lights as belonging to the one and the same larger object that can potentially run us over. I will say a lot more about how learning influences our perceptual processes in Chapter 3. For now, it is enough to see that the enrichment of the input can be learned.

It is important to emphasize that our perceptual apparatus is trying its best to come up with the most probable solution to the task. It is trying to build the most probable three-dimensional model that would project on our retina as the two-dimensional retinal image. But the most probable does not necessarily mean the correct one. Sometimes objects are unusual, and our perceptual system, the function of which is to come up with the most probable perceptual scenario, will come up with the wrong model. Sometimes perception misrepresents (Dretske 1986).

This point is important in order to keep perception apart from the input itself. Perception is not the same as the sensory input. Rather, perception is the elaboration of the sensory input. Perception starts with the sensory input, but it doesn't end there.

More generally, one of the most basic questions one can ask about the mind is what mediates between sensory input and motor output. Light hits my retina, something happens in my skull and then my hand reaches out to grab a cup. But what is it that happens between the input and the output?

The first thing that happens is perceptual processing. The input needs to be transformed into the kind of information that would enable me to reach out in a certain direction. The sensory input gives rise to perceptual processing, which then gives rise to post-perceptual processing, which can be an action or the forming of a belief, for example. In short, perception is perched between sensory input and post-perceptual processing and in order to understand what perception is, we need to delineate it both from sensory input and from post-perceptual processes.

And here the concept of perceptual representation will be crucial. Again, the first thing that needs to happen in the mind is to transform the impoverished and dumb input into a representation of something in the world. Perceptual processing turns sensory input into a perceptual representation. And this concept, the concept of perceptual representation, helps us to understand both how perception differs from sensory input and how it differs from post-perceptual stuff.

1.3 PERCEPTUAL REPRESENTATION

The English word 'apple' represents an apple. As does the French word 'pomme' or the Hungarian word 'alma.' And also a photograph or a painting of an apple. Words and images represent. They can be about something that is not present or maybe doesn't even exist. The word 'unicorn' or a painting of a unicorn represents something that doesn't exist, for example.

Mental states can also represent. They can be about something that is not present or maybe doesn't even exist. When I remember my holiday last summer, this memory represents something that is in the past. When I imagine my next holiday, this imaginative episode represents something that is in the future. And when I think about unicorns, my thought represents something that doesn't even exist. Mental representations are the building blocks of the mind.

The concept of representation has been crucial for the interdisciplinary endeavor of cognitive science, where it serves the purpose of tying together various approaches to understanding the mind (Shea 2018). If mental representations are the building blocks of the mind, then neuroscience, psychology, and philosophy have something in common that they can use in their very different explanatory projects.

In the last section, I said that the task of 3D vision is to come up with the most plausible three-dimensional model of the world on the basis of two pieces of two-dimensional sensory input. Now we can say what it really is that 3D vision gives us: a representation that represents a three-dimensional scene. The task of 3D vision, just like the task of all perceptual processes, is to give us perceptual representations.

More generally, representations attribute certain features to certain things, which is just another way of saying that they represent certain things as having certain features. Or, as philosophers would say, they represent entities as having properties. A photograph of the apple, for example, represents a fist-sized object as having various shape and color properties (assuming it is a color photograph). Similarly, mental representations, and, among mental representations, perceptual representations, also attribute properties to entities: they also represent certain entities as having certain properties. My perceptual representation when I look at an apple also represents this apple as having various shape and color properties.

The range of properties a mental representation attributes is theoretically unlimited. I could have a belief that the apple in front of me was picked by Mr. Smith in an orchard in Brittany on a Tuesday. But the range of properties perceptual representations attribute is much more limited. The property of having been picked by Mr. Smith in an orchard in Brittany on a Tuesday is not a perceptually represented property. It is not something that can be seen or heard when perceiving the apple. Just what properties can be perceptually represented is widely debated in philosophy of perception, with shape, color, spatial location, and size safely in the perceptually represented camp, extravagant properties like having been picked by Mr. Smith in an orchard in Brittany on a Tuesday in the non-perceptual camp, and some controversies about properties like being edible, being fragile, being beautiful or being an apple (Siegel 2006, Bayne 2009, Nanay 2011a, 2012a).

What perceptual representations attribute these properties to is also somewhat controversial. I said that properties are attributed to entities, but what are these entities? Objects would count as entities, and it seems to be a natural description of what happens when I look at an apple to say that my perceptual representation attributes properties to an object: the apple. But perceptual representation can also attribute properties to events: not to unchanging objects, but to the temporal unfolding of a dynamic process. Maybe also to spatiotemporal regions (Clark 2000, Nanay 2022b).

What makes a representation a representation is the possibility that it can misrepresent (Millikan 1984, Dretske 1988). Representations can be incorrect. They can be caused by something and nonetheless be about something else. I may misremember the holiday last year. I remember no mosquitos, but in fact there were many many mosquitos. This amounts to misrepresentation. Or maybe when I think about cats, I think about creatures with three horns. That would also be misrepresentation. And if my visual system comes up with a three-dimensional representation that does not match the actual scene that is in front of me, this would also be misrepresentation.

This gives us a helpful way to keep apart perception and sensory input. Sensory input cannot misrepresent. To simplify a bit, the retinal image is determined by the light that falls on it. It can't be incorrect, in the sense that it slavishly registers the pattern of light that is projected on it (again, this is a simplification – in fact, there is a fair amount of lateral connections between retinal cells that modify retinal processing already, see Section 2.1). Given that sensory input can't misrepresent, it is not a representation.

But perceptual representations can misrepresent. When 3D vision is faced with a very unusual three-dimensional object from an odd angle, it comes up with the most probable three-dimensional scene that would be consistent with the retinal image. However, even if it is the most probable three-dimensional scene, it may not be the one that is actually in front of us. And if it is not, it represents one three-dimensional scene, whereas it is caused by another one. It misrepresents.

Another often-emphasized mark of perceptual representations is perceptual constancy (Burge 2010). Perceptual representations represent distal features of the environment in spite of variations in the proximal input. Hence, the same color may appear different if the illumination conditions are different (and different colors may appear the same if the illumination varies). This is color constancy. Similarly for size and shape constancies: two identical objects can give rise to very different retinal patterns when seen from different distances. When seen from close up, it takes up much of the visual field. When seen from far away, it takes up only a small part of it. And two identical objects project onto our retina very differently when seen from different angles. In Figure 1.1, the projection of the door on our retina is very different in these three examples, but we see the same door in all three cases.

Again, the point here is that the perceptual system does not slavishly register the actual features of the object in front of us. It represents the object's color, size, or shape in a way that is influenced by various other parameters (like the illumination, the distance, or the angle). Sensory input does not show any constancies. Perceptual representations do. So sensory input is not a representation. But perceptual representations are genuine representations.

Perceptual representations are also structured in a different way than beliefs are: perceptual representations are imagistic in some

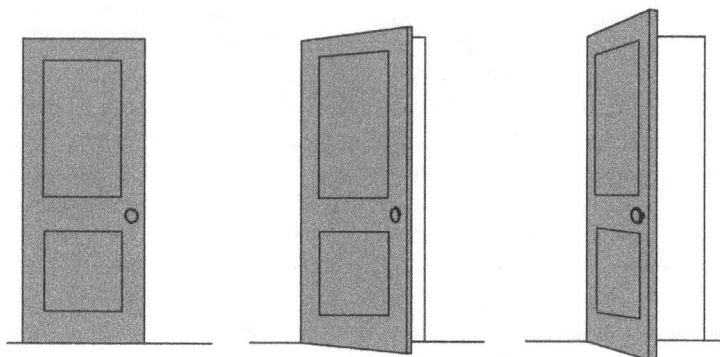

Figure 1.1 Shape constancy.

important sense of the term, whereas beliefs are not: they are propositionally structured (Crane 2009). This distinction, which I will talk about at length in Section 3.1, can help us utilize the concept of perceptual representation to keep perception apart not only from sensory input (what precedes it) but also from belief (which follows it). Unlike sensory input, perception is representational. And unlike belief, it represents imagistically, not propositionally. Again, more on this in Section 3.1.

Note that none of these criteria for representation say anything about whether representations are conscious or not. A crucial assumption of all the sciences of the mind is that mental representations are not necessarily conscious: they may also be unconscious. And the same goes for perceptual representations: they may or may not be conscious.

When you look at an apple, your conscious perceptual experience could be thought of as a representation: your experience represents the apple as red, for example. But that is not the only representation that is involved in seeing an apple. The primary visual cortex (V1) represents some contour properties. And these representations can misrepresent and show perceptual constancies. The same goes for the secondary visual cortex (V2), and further visual areas of the brain, like the V4, the MT, and so on (see Section 2.1 for a more detailed discussion). Neuroscience does not have an awful lot to say about the ways in which conscious perceptual representations represent. But it has a lot to say about the ways in which the primary visual cortex represents contours, for example. But these representations in the primary visual cortex are not conscious. Nor are the ones in V2, V4, or MT. They sometimes (not always) give rise to a conscious percept (see Martinez and Nanay forthcoming), but the norm is that perceptual representations, that is, the building blocks of our perceptual system, are not conscious.

The last couple of decades of perceptual and social psychology gave us plenty of reasons to sideline the concept of consciousness from the study of perception. First, there are the celebrated and headline-making results about the unreliability of our access to our own conscious experiences in general is (Schwitzgebel 2008). So when we are trying to find out about how perception works, it is a bad idea to just introspect how our perceptual experiences feel because such introspective evidence would not just be unscientific, it would also be misleading. One oft-cited example comes from the amount of detail represented in vision. Whenever your eyes are open, it seems as though you see everything sharply, clearly, and in high resolution – as if you had a very good quality cinemascope image of the entire scene in front of you. But vision science teaches us that human vision is much less high-tech (or maybe just much less wasteful). At any moment, you only see a very small part of your surroundings clearly – the approximately two square inch region that your eyes are fixating on (Findlay and Gilchrist 2003). The rest of your visual field is a blurry mess. But because your eyes dart around with great speed and without you noticing, none of your visual field seems blurry. It all seems crystal clear, but it's an illusion. We could reflect on just how crisp an image vision gives us all day in the armchair, but this won't help us figure out how vision works. Our access to our own conscious experience is systematically misleading.

Further, we have a vast amount of evidence that perception can be unconscious: it can guide our actions unconsciously, and it can also prime us unconsciously (Kentridge et al. 1999, Goodale and Milner 2004, Weiskrantz 2009). First, action-guiding perception is often unconscious. When we reach out to grab a cup of coffee, the execution of this action relies on our perceptual states, which represent the size, shape, and spatial location of the cup, for example (see Section 4.2). If I were to perceptually represent the cup a bit further to the left, my reaching movement would be different. Nothing surprising so far. But in one famous set of experiments, in the middle of the performance of the reaching movement, the target was changed – either its spatial location or its size. And this influenced the action execution – the reaching movement changed direction in the course of the execution of this action. Crucially, the subjects are almost always unaware that anything has changed (Goodale et al. 1986, Pelisson et al. 1986, Paulignan et al. 1991). This indicates that the relevant action–guiding perceptual state is unconscious.

Another important set of findings that shows that perception can be unconscious involves unconscious priming: the subject's behavior is altered by the unconsciously presented stimulus. If the perceptual stimulus is masked (quickly followed by another stimulus that prevents the original stimulus from reaching consciousness) or presented for a very short period of time, the subject still perceives it, but has no conscious experience of it (Kouider and Dehaene 2007, there is some dissent on this, see Block and Phillips 2016). If we are presented with the unconscious perceptual stimulus of a picture of a cat, this makes it easier and quicker for us to recognize a (different) picture of a cat. And we are not aware that we have perceived anything cat-related before. There is a large number of findings that show that perception of unconsciously perceived stimulus alters behavior (Dehaene et al. 1998).

More generally, if our aim is to understand perception, this aim should then be neutral to the completely different project of understanding consciousness. The aim is not to understand conscious perception, partly because much of what is interesting about the way our perceptual system works has little to do with consciousness. We want to understand perception, be it conscious or unconscious.

Not everyone in philosophy shares this overall sentiment. Some philosophers focus on conscious perception only and ask what explains the phenomenal character (the conscious feel) of perceptual experiences (Pautz 2010, Schellenberg 2010, Brewer 2011, Logue 2012, French 2018, see, more generally the debates around the merits and demerits of 'naïve realism,' a topic I will not discuss in this book). This is not an uninteresting question, but one that could (and should) be considered secondary. Once we have understood how perception works, we can then, and only then, ask what fancy features some subcategories of perception (namely, conscious perception) have. The question about how perception works is methodologically (and maybe even logically) prior.

1.4 PERCEPTUAL ATTENTION

In many languages, two different words are used to refer to perception. In audition, we have hearing, but also listening. In vision, we have seeing, but also looking. Listening involves some degree of attention as does looking. I don't mean to suggest that somehow our language use reveals great truths about how perception works. Language has evolved to help us understand each other well enough most of the time. So we should not expect language to latch onto the real building blocks of reality, let alone the real building blocks of the mind. But attention is such an integral part of perception that even our very imprecise everyday language picked up on this.

It would be tempting to think of attention as some kind of mental spotlight, which selects some things and leaves others in the dark *after* perception has already done its job. On this view, perception itself has nothing to do with attention, it churns out perceptual representation of both attended and unattended parts of the perceived scene and then once perceptual processing is all over, attention picks out some of them and drops all the others.

This spotlight picture of perception and attention is empirically false (Cave and Bichot 1999, Fazekas and Nanay 2021). Attention does not wait until perception does its job. It interferes with the functioning of the perceptual system at all stages. And this makes a lot of sense in terms of the efficacy of perception. It would be mightily wasteful to create high-resolution perceptual representations of all aspects and all parts of the perceived scene. What attention does is simplify the job our perceptual system faces. It helps perception select those bits of information that we need at that moment. Perceptual processing can ignore all else.

The most famous experiment that shows that the allocation of attention influences perception significantly is the following (Simmons and Chabris 1999). The subjects are given the (not particularly exciting) task to watch a video clip of two teams playing basketball, one dressed in white, and the other dressed in black and count how many passes are completed by the team that is dressed in white. Half of the subjects who complete this task fail to notice that right after the passing begins, a man dressed in a gorilla costume walks into the frame from the left slowly, stands about, makes some funny gestures, and then leaves in a leisurely manner. When subjects watch the same clip without being instructed to count anything, they immediately spot the man in the gorilla costume.

This experiment is part of a larger experimental paradigm with the catchy name of 'inattentional blindness' (Mack and Rock 1998). The general idea is that by not attending to the gorilla, we just plainly fail to see it: we become blind to it. This label highlights the sweeping idea that we do not see what we do not attend to: we only see what we do attend to. While this would do as a slogan, the truth is a bit more nuanced.

One aspect of the gorilla experiment that is not always emphasized is that it only works if the subject counts the passes of the team in white. It does not work if we count the passes of the team in black. Similarly, if we count how many times the team in white passes the ball around, a man dressed in a polar bear costume would be spotted immediately.

Color is crucial because what happens when we don't spot the gorilla in the original experiment is that the black color of the gorilla costume literally melts into the background. Attention is focused on the team in white. Everything else, including the team in black, and very much including the man in the gorilla costume, is discarded by the perceptual system as irrelevant to the task. Does this mean that we are strictly speaking blind to what we are not attending to? Maybe not (Wolfe 1999, but see Rees et al. 1999). But the perceptual system treats whatever we are not attending to as mere noise.

Attention comes in many forms, but the most important distinction for now (more to come in Section 6.2) is between overt and covert attention. Shifting your attention from the chair to the carpet can happen in two ways. You could just move your eyes from the chair to the carpet. This is called an overt shift of attention. But you can also shift your attention without moving your eyes at all. So you're still fixing your eyes on the chair, but you shift your attention to the carpet. This is called a covert shift of attention (Posner 1980, Posner et al. 1984).

Overt attention makes a pretty heavy-duty interference in our perceptual processing. By moving our eyes, we change the sensory input. What was sharp and in focus at the middle of the retina is now a blurry mess, and what was almost unrecognizable at the periphery of our visual field is now in focus and crystal clear. By changing the input, overt shifts of attention change the determinacy of what is processed perceptually.

But covert shifts of attention are even more interesting from this point of view. A typical experimental task in the covert shift of attention paradigm is to fixate on a cross in the middle of the screen and, while keeping your eyes there in the middle, shift your attention to the left or to the right (where there are some other visual displays). And the main finding is that those visual displays that are attended to are represented in a higher degree of determinacy (Yeshurun and Carrasco 1998). And experiments of this kind can also help us to figure out at what stage of perceptual processing attentional interference happens. It turns out that it happens at all possible levels, including the very earliest ones (in the primary visual cortex, for example, in the case of vision, see Dugue et al. 2020).

A philosophical gloss of these findings is that attention increases the determinacy of perceptual representations (Nanay 2010a, 2011c, Stazicker 2011). A widely used distinction in philosophy is between determinate and determinable properties (Funkhouser 2006). Determinate properties are more specific and determinables are less specific. Red is a determinable of scarlet, and it is the determinate of the property of being colored. Thus, the determinable–determinate distinction gives us a hierarchy of properties, from the most determinable ones (like being colored) to the most determinate ones (like a specific shade of scarlet).

When I talked about perceptual representations, I described them as representations that attribute properties (to an entity). But then the question is: what kind of properties are being attributed here: determinates or determinables? (see also the debate about perceptual confidence here, Morrison 2016, Munton 2017, Nanay 2020c). And the answer is that this depends on the allocation of attention. Attention increases (or at least tries to increase) the determinacy of the perceptually represented properties. So those features that you are attending to will be more determinate than the rest. This is very clear in the case of peripheral vision, where details in the periphery of the visual field can only be very sparse, whereas foveal vision (vision at the middle of the visual field) has great accuracy. But it is also true of covert attention, as the experiments presented above show.

According to this picture, perceptual representation is constituted by the attributed properties and just what kind of properties (determinables or determinates) are attributed depends on attention. The content of perceptual representations very much depends on the allocation of attention.

Note that nothing in this account presupposes that attention is conscious. Just like perceptual representations may be conscious or unconscious, perceptual attention may also be conscious or unconscious – as it has been demonstrated by a number of experimental findings.

Maybe the most famous of these is a study where a picture of a naked woman is presented in a way that it could not be consciously perceived because it was presented for an extremely short period of time (Jiang et al. 2006). It showed up in either the bottom right or the top left corner of the screen. After this initial presentation (of which the experimental subjects noticed nothing) comes a simple object-recognition task: everyday objects, again presented either top left or bottom right, needed to be identified.

The surprising finding is that the very same object was recognized more easily and quickly when it appeared at the part of the screen where attention had been drawn by the (unconsciously seen) picture of the nude. Because of the naked lady, attention was lingering on that part of the scene and that made it easier and quicker to recognize objects presented there. And the subjects had no idea that their attention was drawn there (and no idea why). In case there is any doubt that it was the unconscious presentation of the naked lady that did the trick, this effect was far more significant for heterosexual men, than for homosexual men or heterosexual women, indicating that the nude picture itself was grabbing the subjects' attention without them noticing it.

Attention is often taken to be a simple selection process, that is, the screening out of irrelevant information, but things are a bit more complicated. In probably the most famous characterization of attention, William James said this:

> Everyone knows what attention is. It is the taking possession by the mind, in clear and vivid form, of one out of what seem several simultaneously possible objects or trains of thought.
>
> (James 1890, p. 403)

First of all, I really don't think everyone knows what attention (or, for that matter any other mental phenomenon) is. But the main problem with this characterization is that attention is more than just selection. It is not just that those features we are not attending to are not processed further. The perceptual processing of those features that we are attending to is cranked up. So attention does not merely ignore irrelevant information. It also amplifies relevant information (Fazekas and Nanay 2021, see Watzl 2017 for a contrasting take).

The take-home message is that attention is very much part of the perceptual apparatus: it is not something that happens after perception has finished, but perception itself involves attention.

This may be a good place to talk about the relation between perception and emotion. Our attention is often captured by emotionally salient stimuli. In fact, this is a feature of perceptual attention that perceptual psychologists routinely take advantage of in their research: seeing a scary tiger grabs your attention in a way seeing an empty coffee cup does not. And given that attention is heavily involved in perceptual representation, emotion must be as well (I will use the concept of emotion here, but those who make a distinction between emotions and affective states more generally, which would include moods, desires and any states with affective valence, could read 'affective' instead of 'emotional' in what follows).

This way in which perception and emotion are intertwined has also been emphasized by empirical research. Take, for example, perceptual learning. Perceptual learning is the psychological phenomenon in which perceiving a certain kind of stimulus leaves a mark on the perceptual system, so the next time you perceive a similar kind of stimulus, your perception of it will be different (see Section 3.2 for more on perceptual learning).

We know a fair amount about the neural mechanisms behind perceptual learning and how it often happens in the earliest stages of perceptual processing. The crucial finding from our point of view here is that perceptual learning involving emotionally salient stimuli is much more efficient and much quicker (Murphy 1956). Unless we take perception itself to be emotionally charged, this would be difficult to explain: emotion-free perception would need to trigger our emotions, which then, in turn, would need to influence the early cortical processing. This would amount to lengthy processing, where first the early cortical representation is induced by means of the sensory input, which, in turn, activates a higher-level emotional state, which takes time, which then, in turn, activates the early cortical regions again in a top-down manner, to induce perceptual learning. It is difficult to see how this long and cumbersome way of inducing perceptual learning would be more efficient than the entirely early cortical matter of emotion-free perceptual learning, where the early cortical representation induces perceptual learning directly.

Seeing an angry tiger has a very negative emotional charge, or as it is often said, emotional valence. Seeing a photograph of your romantic partner probably has a positive valence. And I used the example of seeing an empty coffee cup as an example of neutral valence. But it has been argued that there is no such thing as completely neutral valence. Even stimuli like an empty coffee cup have what is often referred to as 'microvalences' (Lebrecht et al. 2012). In short, perception is an emotional affair through and through.

1.5 THE FUNCTION OF PERCEPTION

Perception is an extremely costly mental capacity. About 50% of the cortex is devoted to vision, and that is not counting the other sense modalities. Perception, then, must confer enormous evolutionarily benefits that would explain why we organisms with such costly mechanisms had a selective advantage.

But what is it that perception is supposed to do? What is the function of perception? In biology and the philosophy of biology, function is a key concept. The human heart pumps blood and it also makes loud thumping noises. The function of the heart is to pump blood. It is not the function of the heart to make loud thumping noises. The reason for this is that pumping blood contributes to survival, whereas making loud thumping noises does not.

There are various debates surrounding the concept of function that we can safely bracket here. Is it past survival that fixes function or is it determined by what would happen in counterfactual situations, if things were a little different? (Millikan 1984, Nanay 2010c). In other words, is function determined by what happened to those hearts that did not pump blood or by what would happen if the heart didn't pump blood? For the purposes of this book, the most important thing is that our perceptual system is an evolved mechanism just like our heart. It does many things. But, like with the heart, only some of these things constitute our selective advantage.

And here the crucial insight is that what matters for survival is, on the face of it, what we do. If we do things that help us get fed and protect us from predators, we survive. If we do things that leave us hungry and make us easy prey for predators, we die. So action has a very clear selective advantage. The selective advantage of perception is not so clear.

But the selective advantage of acting in accordance with our needs can help us to understand the evolutionary perks of perception. In order to act in a way that enhances survival, one needs to represent the world as being a certain way. You can't approach the food if you have no idea where the food is in relation to you – on the left, on the right or in front of you. And you can't run away from predators unless you represent their whereabouts – and keep on representing their whereabouts as they move closer or further away from you. In short, perception helps us to act in a way that contributes to our selective advantage.

What matters for survival is action, but what makes action successful or unsuccessful is perception. This explains why it pays off to burn up so much energy maintaining our perceptual apparatus. Organisms with a worse, slower, less precise, perceptual apparatus are more likely to get eaten by predators and less likely to find scarce resources. The function of perception is to help us act successfully (Nanay forthcoming a). The function of perception is to guide action.

But that is not all. While the importance of action-guiding perception is difficult to deny, this is not the only function perception has. Some evolved mechanisms have more than one function. As we shall see in Section 2.4, the hairlike endings of the olfactory receptive cells in our nasal cavity have the function to pick up olfactory signals while sniffing, but they also have the function to pick up flavor signals when swallowing food, for example. Or, to go with a more prosaic example, our tongue has the function to taste flavors and also to help us in vocalizing.

Perception also has more than one function. It has the function to guide actions. But it also has the function to help us form non-perceptual representations. We have seen that running away from predators is an action that usually contributes to our evolutionary fitness. Those who don't manage to run away get eaten and their genes won't show up in the next generation. And the action of running away is greatly helped by the ability to perceive where the predator is and how it moves. But knowing which direction to run away from is not enough to not get eaten. We also need to know what creatures we need to run away from. And this is where non-perceptual representations come in handy.

In order to successfully run away from predators and approach food, it is not enough to know what direction to run from or toward. We also need to be able to tell the predator and the food source apart. We also need to know what strategy to apply in the case of different predators (and different food sources). And here non-perceptual representations can help immensely. If you know that predator A can run fast for a short while but then runs out of breath, you need a different strategy to escape from what would be successful in the case of the slow and steady predator B. You need to recognize the difference between predator A and predator B and then you need to apply this information to choose an escape strategy. While some of this process is clearly perceptual, not all of it is. The success of an action is not determined exclusively by the perceptual process that guides it. Even if your perceptual system is amazing at keeping track of how your prey moves and at helping you capture it, if your non-perceptual representation gets the target wrong – for example, not figuring out that the prey is poisonous – then the amazingly executed action still leads to your demise.

But these non-perceptual representations were also formed at earlier stages of our lives with the help of the perceptual system. The reason you know what kind of action is the best in the case of predator A and predator B is likely to be that you have observed them before. To use the term 'belief,' for convenience, as a placeholder to refer to non-perceptual representation – but see also Section 4.1 for more on the concept of belief – we can say that your earlier perceptual states helped you form beliefs and now it is these beliefs that help your action to contribute to your survival. Perception, in this case, contributes to survival indirectly – via belief formation.

So perception has the function to guide our actions and to help us form true beliefs (which then also help us perform actions successfully). But couldn't perception have some further functions? Perception is also often – not always – accompanied by a certain phenomenal feel: looking at a red apple brings on a certain reddish phenomenal character.

Is this yet another function of perception? No. First of all, if some, but not all perceptual states have phenomenology, then it is not a very good candidate for being the function of perception. Of course, function is not always fulfilled. The sperm, for example, has the function to fertilize the egg, but very few sperms will actually fulfill this function. But note the disanalogy between these two cases: those sperms that fail to fertilize the egg do the exact same things as the sperms that succeed. It's just that in the vast majority of cases, only one sperm gets to fertilize one egg. But regardless of what theory of consciousness we endorse, conscious perception is substantially different from unconscious one, whereas the sperms that get wasted and the sperms that manage to fertilize the egg are not substantially different. So it is still puzzling how and why perception would have the function to have a conscious phenomenal feel when many (even most) perceptual states are not phenomenally conscious and, crucially, very often (e.g., in the case of action-guiding vision, see Chapter 4), it is not the kind of mental state that can become conscious.

This is not to say that consciousness is useless, and a mere gloss on top of our mental apparatus (although this view has its own merits). I want to remain neutral about the function of consciousness (if it indeed has any). And that includes the function of the consciousness of perceptual states. It may be the case that when a perceptual state is conscious, this conscious phenomenal feel increases the speed or the accuracy of perceptual processing, for example. But this claim, if it is true (and the jury is very much out on claims of this kind), is a claim about the function of consciousness, not about the function of perception. And this chapter is not about the function of consciousness, but about the function of perception. While perception has the function to help us perform actions and also to help us form correct beliefs, it does not appear to have the function to provide us with vivid phenomenal feel as it is not clear how conscious perception would contribute to our selective advantage more than unconscious perception – either directly or even indirectly.

More generally, it should be noted that the function of perception has little to do with consciousness. If perception can help me get away from the predator, it helps us regardless of whether I am aware of various features of this predator. Both conscious and unconscious perception would do. In fact, we now know that in the case of the majority of our perceptually guided actions, the perceptual process that is involved is not conscious – see Section 4.3 for discussion. And the same considerations apply to forming non-perceptual representations, although here there is a bit more space for disagreement, see Section 3.5.

Thus far, I have treated perception as a monolithic phenomenon: it is the processing of sensory input, which gives us perceptual representations. But perception is a remarkably diverse phenomenon and depending on what this sensory input is, the processing thereof is of a very different kind. And this leads to very different kinds of perceptual representations. Seeing a foggy landscape requires very different perceptual processes from smelling a burnt pizza. This is the topic I turn to in the next chapter.

1.6 SUMMARY

Perception is more than the mere sensory input – it is the elaboration or embellishment of this input in the service of cognition and action. This raises two immediate questions: how can we keep perception apart from sensory stimulation and how can we keep perception apart from postperceptual (cognitive) processing? Perception comes after sensory input and before cognition and in order to zoom in on perception, we need to differentiate it from both of these.

Perception represents the world and one question I address in this chapter is how it does so. Beliefs also represent the world, but they represent it very differently from the way perception does. Special emphasis is given to how attention influences perceptual processing and how specifying the content of perceptual representations needs to take the allocation of perceptual attention into consideration.

THE VARIETY OF SENSES

2.1 VISION

The previous chapter was about perception in general, but the vast majority of my examples came from vision. When I noticed this while re-reading an earlier draft, I changed the examples to be evenly distributed between seeing, hearing, smelling, tasting, and touching. But it came across as extremely forced, so I changed it all back.

Humans are visuocentric creatures: we devote more attention to visual perception than to other sense modalities. But this should not make us privilege vision when it comes to the understanding of perception in general. In other species, vision has less of a monopoly on perception. Dogs have fairly poor vision and very good olfaction, for example. Just because humans happen to rely on vision more than on other sense modalities, we should not take vision to be perception par excellence. In fact, in many ways, vision is a fairly atypical form of perception.

We receive information perceptually via a number of sense modalities. Traditionally, five such sense modalities are distinguished: seeing, hearing, smelling, tasting, and touching. But as we shall see, these ways of perceiving are not as easily distinguished from one another as one may think.

DOI: 10.4324/9781032639536-2

An important reason why it is tempting to take vision to be the paradigmatic case of perception is that we just know more about the way vision works than about any of the other sense modalities.

In terms of anatomy, visual processing starts with the light hitting our retina. The retinal cells pick up the brightness and color information from the light that projects onto the retina. The retinal image, then, is a close to exact replica of the two-dimensional projection of the visual scene in front of us. I said 'close to exact' because some adjustments are made already in retinal processing: if neighboring retinal cells react in radically different ways, corrections are made (Thoreson et al. 2008). But by and large, the retinal image could be thought of as the two-dimensional projection of the visual scene in front of us.

This two-dimensional image (or, rather, two slightly different two-dimensional images from the retina of the two eyes) is then sent to the primary visual cortex (V1) via the lateral geniculate nucleus (LGN) (Grill-Spector and Malach 2004, Van Essen 2004, Katzner and Weigelt 2013). The reason why we know a fair amount about the neuroscience of vision is that we have a fairly clear idea about how the primary visual cortex works. Crucially, the primary visual cortex is retinotopic: it is homomorphic with the retina, which just means that it is something like an inexact copy of the retinal image. In other words, the V1 is organized in the same way as the retina: if there is a small triangle projected at the top left corner of the retina, there will be a roughly triangle-shaped activation at the upper left corner of the primary visual cortex. If the triangle then moves across the retina to the bottom right corner, the same thing happens in the primary visual cortex (Grill-Spector and Malach 2004).

The primary visual cortex is located at the back of our head and while there are significant differences in terms of its size and location across individuals, for any given individual, with a couple of hours of work, we can locate the primary visual cortex fairly accurately with the help of fMRI technology. The main perk of fMRI in comparison with other brain imaging techniques is that it is extremely fine-grained. So if in complete darkness a single red dot is flashed in the middle of your visual field, this can be picked up quite accurately with the help of fMRI imaging in the primary visual cortex. By moving this dot around and seeing what part of the primary visual cortex gets activated (which here means where blood-flow increases slightly), we can map out the primary visual cortex.

Whatever is projected on the retina serves as the input to the primary visual cortex. But the visual cortex does much more. If a dotted line is projected on the retina, the primary visual cortex connects the dots and represents a line. If the Kanizsa triangle (see Figure 2.1) is projected on the retina, the primary visual cortex represents an actual triangle (Kok et al. 2016).

One helpful metaphor used by neuroscientists to describe the earliest stages of visual processing, that is, the early visual cortices (and especially the primary visual cortex) is that of an 'active blackboard' (Girard et al. 2001, Bullier 2001, 2004, Sterzer et al. 2006, Roelfsema and de Lange 2016). The general idea is that V1 functions as a blackboard. Various processes can write on this blackboard. Sensory – that is, retinal – input automatically leaves traces on this blackboard, and

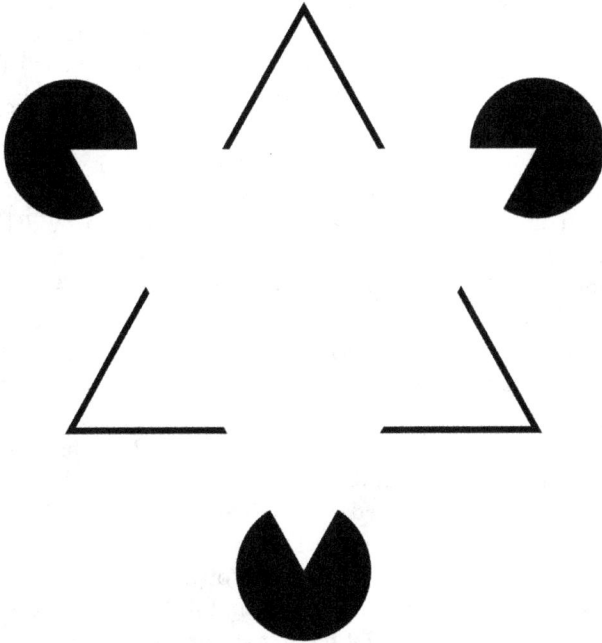

Figure 2.1 The Kanizsa triangle (CC BY-SA 3.0).

does so in a retinotopic manner. To simplify a bit, what is on the retina is copied onto the blackboard.

But there are other processes that can draw on this blackboard. Some of them are determined by the sensory stimulation that shows up in other parts of the blackboard (as in the case of the Kanizsa triangle). Some are determined by perceptual processing in a different sense modality (see Section 2.5). And in some other cases, the drawing is done by mechanisms further up in visual processing (see Section 3.2, see also Mechelli et al. 2004, Dentico et al. 2014).

The primary visual cortex represents contours: it breaks up the undifferentiated image provided by the retina into smaller units, divided by edges and contours. And this information is sent on to a number of other early cortical regions, for example, V2, V3, V4/V8, V5/MT). These are all thought to be specialized (at least to a certain extent) for specific kinds of properties. V4/V8, for example, represents color, V5/MT represents movement, and so on. These distinctions should not be taken to be too sharp: V1, for example, also processes color information and V4/V8 also does a fair amount of shape processing. What is crucial, however, is that all these visual areas are retinotopic: we get layers of largely overlapping images highlighting more and more features of the retinal input: contours, edges, colors, movement, and segregated areas.

I argued in Section 1.3 that the representation of all of these features count as genuine perceptual representations. And here is a demonstration. Look at Figure 2.2a. Seems like an abstract figure, not depicting anything. Now look at Figure 2.2b. And look at Figure 2.2a again. The image looks very different now. The difference in your experience is salient enough. But what matters for us here is that the activation in the primary visual cortex is also very different before and after you looked at Figure 2.2b. Take the region around the dolphin's eye. Before you looked at Figure 2.2b, that region of your primary visual cortex did very little. It is a monochrome black patch, after all. V1 represented it as a monochrome empty patch. After looking at Figure 2.2b, however, the direction-sensitive neurons of V1 that correspond to the contours of the eye are firing feverishly (Teufel et al. 2018). This is a beautiful demonstration of how V1 does not merely slavishly register whatever is projected on the retina. It brings in all available resources in order to come up with an

Figure 2.2a What's in this picture? (Image courtesy of Christoph Teufel).

Figure 2.2b The reveal (Image courtesy of Christoph Teufel).

accurate representation of the perceived scene. I will come back to this example in Section 3.2 and in Section 6.3.

The visual processing in these areas (V1, V2, V3, V4/V8, V5/MT) is often referred to as early vision. But visual processing does not stop with early vision. Early vision breaks down the mass of visual information into contours, regions and eventually to visual objects – objects that can move and take their features with them.

And of course these nested representations along the hierarchy of perceptual processing eventually give rise to a three-dimensional model of the scene in front of us. This aspect of visual processing is, again, something we understand fairly well: how the slight differences between the retinal image coming from the left eye and the retinal image coming from the right eye are exploited by the visual system to have a clearer idea of what the three-dimensional structure of the perceived scene may be.

Another crucial source of information the visual system relies on when constructing a three-dimensional model on the basis of two-dimensional input concerns occlusion: (non-transparent) objects that are closer to us occlude objects that are further away from us. And occlusion has very simple visual markers. For example, a T-shape junction of edges is something that is very easily detectable – already in V1 (von der Heydt and Zhang 2018). But in everyday scenes, a T-junction very often indicates occlusion: the region with the border that includes the horizontal line of the T occludes the regions that have the border that includes the vertical line of the T. This is just one simple way in which the scene-segmentation in terms of edges and contours already carries a lot of 3D information.

One odd feature of visual perception is that in the scene in front of us, some objects are very likely to be partially occluded by others. So when you are looking out of the window, the tree is half-occluded by the car that is parked in front of it, but the car itself is partly occluded by a fire hydrant, and so on. And if there is a mosquito-net on your window, the little threads of the net occlude a fair chunk of the visual scene in front of you. Nonetheless, you somehow perceptually represent these objects not as truncated by other objects in front of them. You don't see a half-tree or a half-car. You see the entire tree, which happens to be partially occluded by the car and the entire car, which happens to be partially occluded by the fire hydrant.

One of the tricky maneuvers that the visual system performs all the time is to come up with the occluded part of objects on the basis of the non-occluded parts. This is called amodal completion, which, in the visual sense modalities, is defined as the representation of occluded parts of perceived objects.

Crucially, amodal completion is a genuinely perceptual phenomenon. It does not happen post-perceptually, but as part of the functioning of the visual system. We know from a number of experiments that visual completion happens very early in visual processing, already in the primary visual cortex (Lee and Nguyen 2001, Thielen et al. 2019). Take Figure 2.3. If you are looking at the image in the middle, your visual system completes this as the figure on the left and not as the figure on the right. And in your primary visual cortex, the direction-sensitive neurons along the illusory contour of the figure on the left are firing, whereas the ones along the illusory contour of the figure on the right don't.

It is difficult to overstate just how widely our visual system relies on amodal completion (Michotte and Burke 1951, Nanay 2018b). Just try to imagine a not digitally manipulated visual scene where there is no occlusion whatsoever. Not easy. And even in most of these we get what is sometimes referred to as self-occlusion: when we look at a cube in front of a homogenous white background, there is still amodal completion of the backside of the cube – the side that is facing away from us (Ekroll et al. 2016). Amodal completion is not a visual curiosity – it is the default (see Section 5.2 for more on amodal completion). It is one of the many ways in which the visual system builds a complex representation on the basis of very little information in the retinal input.

The last distinctive feature of vision I want to talk about concerns eye movements. As we have seen in Section 1.3, when you look

Figure 2.3 Amodal completion.

around, it seems as though you see everything sharply, clearly, and in high resolution. But vision science teaches us that what actually happens is that at any given moment, you only see a very small part of your surroundings clearly – the approximately two square inch region on which your eyes are fixating. Because your eyes dart around with great speed and without you noticing, none of your visual field seems blurry. The reason we know that our vision does not actually present us with a high-resolution Technicolor cinemascope image is that we can infer this from how our vision works in more unusual circumstances (e.g., when we can't move our eyes at all).

In order for there to be visual perception, we need eye movements. Some of these eye movements, which are called *saccades*, are relatively slow (about 5 per second). They can be voluntarily triggered and could span across great distances in your visual field, say, from all the way to the right to all the way to the left (Kowler et al. 1995). But the other, equally important form of eye movements is called *micro-saccades*, which are much more frequent, not consciously controllable and stay relatively close to the fixation point. Without micro-saccades, there is no visual input at all. If the eye is completely stabilized, so that it is incapable of performing micro-saccades, there is no visual input at all – you don't see anything (Coppola and Purves 1996). In short, eye movements are a constitutive part of visual perception (see Section 4.4 for more on this).

2.2 AUDITION

Vision is only one of the sense modalities. While humans are visuocentric creatures, we also get information from non-visual sense modalities, especially from audition. While our hearing is not as good as that of some other mammals, for example, cats, elephants or horses, we do rely on it significantly. In Section 2.1, I warned against generalizing too much from vision to all the other sense modalities. And audition is a case in point. Audition, in many respects, works very differently from vision.

Vision is very good at providing us with large amounts of spatial details of relatively stable scenes. Audition is not very good at this. But audition is very good at something else, namely, temporal resolution. One somewhat simplified way of thinking about vision and audition is that vision gives us a spatially very specific, but temporally not very specific representation and audition gives us the converse: representation that is temporally very specific and spatially not so much. I say that this picture is simplified because audition is in fact surprisingly good at providing spatial representation, especially given the scarcity of spatial information of the auditory input.

Remember the analogy, from Section 1.2, of figuring out the location, speed and size of ships on the basis of the movement of two pieces of cloth at the end of two narrow canals connected to the lake. That is exactly what audition does: deciphers a huge amount of information about events around us on the basis of the movement of our eardrums.

Vision has a hell of a problem to solve: putting together a 3D model of the scene in front of us on the basis of 2D projections. But in some sense, that is a piece of cake compared to coming up with a 3D model of the scene not just in front of us, but behind us and all around us and not just its momentary state, but also the way it changes. And all that on the basis of the extremely impoverished input of sound waves hitting our eardrums.

So vision is clearly different from audition, but how exactly are they different? More generally, how should we characterize the difference between the different sense modalities (Grice 1962, Macpherson 2014)? Is vision different from audition because they 'feel' different? Seeing the fireworks has a reddish feel, but hearing it has a loud feel. That is one difference. Another difference is the sense organs used. The sense organ of vision is the eye. Audition uses the ears. That is another difference. Yet another one is about the brain regions involved in vision and audition (the visual and the auditory cortices respectively, which work very differently). Or is it about the features that vision and audition are sensitive to? Vision is sensitive to colors, audition is not.

While it may seem that we have many good ways of keeping the sense modalities apart, on closer inspection none of these ways of differentiating between them is unproblematic. Appealing to conscious feel is odd in the light of the fact that both vision and audition can be unconscious. Appealing to the differences of the sense organ may seem obvious, maybe too obvious, but when it comes to the other senses, things get more complicated, as we shall see in Section 2.4. But even the seemingly trivial claim that we see with our eyes and hear with our ears is far from being obvious.

A celebrated technique developed to help blind people navigate their environment is the so-called sensory substitution device. The blind person has a camera installed on their head and the images are transformed in real time to a fairly complex auditory or tactile stimulus. In the case of tactile stimulus, this can be little pricks on a small rectangle-shaped part of the skin (or the tongue) that would spatially correspond to the recorded image. In the case of audition, this transformation is a bit more complicated as the two spatial dimensions of the visual input are not transferred to two spatial dimensions of tactile input, but rather to pitch and loudness coordinates. So a dot in the upper left corner would correspond to a high-pitched loud tune, and so on. As this auditory stimulus tracks, in real time, the image recorded by the camera, subjects can navigate complex terrains and they often even report their perceptual experiences in terms of occlusion – one object partly occluded behind another – which is something vision can represent, but audition can't (Bach-y-Rita and Kercel 2003). Is this sensory substituted perception vision or audition then? Not an easy question to answer. If we go by sense organs, it's audition. If we go by phenomenology, it's vision. So do these subjects see with their eyes and hear with their ears? It's not at all clear that they do.

Going by brain regions will not work either given the remarkable plasticity of the brain: those parts of the brain that are not used or used less are reallocated to perform other functions. The auditory cortices of deaf individuals, for example, can take on all kinds of other functions that have nothing to do with hearing. Finally, while it is true that by and large vision and audition are sensitive to different features, there are some features that both of them are sensitive to, for example, spatial location. And when it comes to vision and touch, for example, there is a substantial overlap between the features they are sensitive to (e.g., shape and texture, see Green 2022).

In short, there is no easy answer to the question of how we should individuate sense modalities. But this question may not be as important to understanding perception as it has been taken to be in the history of philosophy. Vision is clearly different from audition, but at the end of the day, the visual and the auditory systems work together to come up with a correct representation of the world around us. Vision is good at some things, audition is good at others. Crucially, the two systems interact at almost all parts of the process, even at the earliest stages. There are strong lateral links between the visual and the auditory cortices, so much so that auditory information can be decoded from the visual cortex alone (Vetter et al. 2014). But this cross-talk happens already at extremely early stages of processing. For example, our eye movements systematically and directly influence the movement of our eardrums (Gruters et al. 2018).

We have seen that early visual processing is retinotopic: there is a spatial correspondence between the retina and the early visual representations. And there is something similar going on in audition as well. Here, early auditory representations are tonotopic, which means that there is a correspondence between the pitch of the stimulus and the region of the auditory cortex, where this stimulus is processed. To simplify considerably, we can think of the auditory cortex as the keyboard of a piano, where two tones that have similar pitch are processed in adjacent parts of the auditory cortex.

Just like vision, audition gives us representations of the world around us. It attributes properties to things. Two questions arise: what are the auditory properties that are attributed and what are they attributed to?

Some unquestioned candidates for auditory properties are pitch and loudness. But it is less clear whether some other properties are auditorily represented. We have seen a version of this question in Section 1.3. The reason why this is an especially important question about the auditory sense modality is speech perception. One big debate in philosophy of perception is whether semantic properties of human speech are auditorily represented or whether they are represented post-auditorily, on the basis of the auditory representation of pitch and loudness (Smith 2009, Brogaard 2018).

When I hear you saying 'I don't know,' what is represented auditorily? It seems clear that the pitch and loudness of your voice are auditorily represented, but audition does more than that. It also segments this approximately one-second-long stimulus into bits that are then processed as units. It is segmented into three units, roughly corresponding to 'I,' 'don't' and 'know.' But the flow of auditory information does not have natural breaks between these units. This sentence very rarely sounds like 'I ... [pause] ... don't ...[pause] ... know.' It is one continuous string of auditory stimuli, but the auditory system already breaks it down to words. This is strong evidence that speech properties are represented in audition.

Maybe some would be tempted to think that only pitch and loudness properties are represented in audition, with speech properties added on later in post-perceptual processing. After all, speech is part of the domain of linguistic cognition, which could be thought to be radically different from the domain of perception. As we shall see in great detail in Section 3.4, this opposition between linguistic and perceptual processing is without any factual basis, as the two are intertwined in all kinds of interesting ways. And this intertwining is especially important in the case of audition as there seems to be plenty of evidence that the processing of semantic properties of speech heavily influences, and is heavily influenced by, already extremely early processing in the primary auditory cortex (A1).

I talked about the properties represented in auditory perception. But what are these auditory properties attributed to? When I hear a car crash in front of my house, what is it that I hear? The actual event of the crash? The sound of the crash? Or maybe the spatiotemporal region where the crash takes place? (O'Callaghan 2007, Nudds 2010, Young and Nanay 2022b).

It seems that sometimes auditory properties, like pitch and loudness, are attributed, or bound, to sounds. After all, it is a sound that has pitch and loudness, not the car crash itself. And this is indeed the dominant view of audition: we hear sounds. But this leaves open the question about what sounds actually are. Are they to be identified with the soundwaves coming from an auditory event? Or with the event (in the case of the car crash, the collision between the two cars) that produces these soundwaves? Maybe something else? (Kulvicki 2008, Leddington 2019).

Further, it is not at all clear that sound is the only plausible candidate for what properties are attributed to in audition. When you're trying to kill a mosquito at night in your hotel room, your auditory system attributes properties (above all, spatial location properties) to it that allow your motor system to slap it successfully (Cohen 2010, Nanay 2013). These properties are not attributed to the sound of the mosquito, after all, you don't want to slap the sound of the mosquito, but the mosquito itself. It seems that at least in this case, auditory properties are attributed, or bound, to the actual object and not the sound thereof.

But the example of slapping the mosquito in the dark hotel room is important for another reason as well and that has to do with the old question of representing space. As we have seen, audition provides much less spatial information than vision. At least in humans. The auditory system of other animals can represent spatial location with great specificity. But the human auditory system can't. This should not mislead us to think audition does not represent spatial information. It surely does, as anyone who has observed the way a cat's ears move as a result of the various noises around it would know (see also Young 2017 on the ways in which audition represents spatial information in humans).

We have seen that there is a tendency in the literature to take vision to be the paradigmatic example of perception. Focusing on the quirks and specificities of audition could be a good way of questioning the primacy of vision in our thinking about perception. But we should be careful not to replace visuo-centrism with audiovisuo-centrism. Perception is not vision, but perception is not vision + audition either. There are many other ways in which we get perceptual information from our environment, each with its own specificities and quirks.

2.3 TOUCH

In some sense, touch is a more basic sense modality than either vision or audition. Simple organisms like the sea slug have no vision or audition, but if we can describe them as perceiving their environment (and many would argue that we should), they perceive their environment by means of tactile perception – touch (Fulkerson 2014).

But touch has an odd and somewhat surprising other form of primacy among the sense modalities and this has to do with what senses we trust. Remember the story of one of Jesus's twelve disciples, Thomas? After Jesus died, Thomas saw his wounds, but he did not believe they were there until he touched them with his own hands. And it has been shown experimentally that people take tactile perception to be more reliable than visual or other perceptual information (Fairhurst et al. 2018). Given that, in some sense, touch brings us closer to the object, this may not even be that surprising.

While touch has been taken to be one of the five sense modalities ever since ancient Greek times, it is itself not a unified phenomenon. We need to make at least two different distinctions.

First, tactile perception works very differently depending on what we do. You can actively explore something by touch, for example, when you reach into your bag to look for the keys or when you run your fingers through your loved one's hair. In this case, the tactile perceptual system registers the change in tactile stimulus as your hand moves.

But this is not the only way touch can give us information about the world (Matthen 2021). When you hold out the palm of your hand and I press a coin against it, this is a very different form of tactile perception. The tactile input changes here as well, but it does not change as a result of what you do (but rather as a result of what I do). Active tactile exploration gives us a very different set of tactile features, which often makes it easier for tactile perception to represent distal features of the environment.

Remember that I said (in Section 1.3) that perception represents distal features. But at least on the face of it, touch blatantly fails to do so. We can only touch things that are in contact with our skin. In this sense at least, tactile perception does not represent anything distal. Note the disanalogy with vision and audition. Vision can give us information about things that are far away from us. Audition too. But tactile perception works differently. How can we then call tactile perceptual representations genuine representations?

One way of making this point even more urgent is to go back to the topic of perceptual constancies. Perceptual constancies represent distal features in the face of changes in proximal features. So when we see a red door, our visual system represents it as having the distal color red in spite of variations in how the top of the door, as it is in shadow, appears almost black, and the bottom, illuminated by strong sunshine, appears almost yellow.

But are there perceptual constancies when it comes to touch? There are, at least when it comes to the 'active exploration' sense of touch. When I run my fingers along a wire fence, my tactile perception represents distal features, the whole mash of the wire fence and not just the one wire I happen to be in tactile contact with at the moment, given the temporally unfolding nature of this form of tactile perception.

Note, however, that the relation between the distal features that are represented and the proximal features that serve as input is much tighter in tactile perception than in vision or audition. And this, in turn, may explain why we tend to trust our tactile perception more than our vision or audition.

Another aspect of the differences between vision and tactile perception is highlighted by the so-called Molyneux's question. Suppose that a congenitally blind subject (someone blind from birth) is familiar with two very differently shaped objects by tactile perception. If her vision were restored would she immediately be able to tell them apart and identify them visually? So our blind subject handles a cube and a sphere and then when her sight is restored, she looks at a cube and a sphere, can she identify one as a sphere and the other one as a cube by sight alone (see Degenaar 1996 on the history of Molyneux's question and Evans 1985, Campbell 2005, Levin 2008, Matthen and Cohen 2020, Nanay 2020b for more contemporary takes).

This was a theoretical question in the 17th century, when it was originally raised and it still was at the turn of the century. But it has been suggested that the question can be answered, given today's medical technology, in an empirical manner. We can now, in some circumstances, restore the sight of congenitally blind people (Held et al. 2011). And after this operation, the subjects could immediately match one visual shape with another one, but they could not match the shapes across sense modalities – which would have been the task at stake in the Molyneux debate. They did manage to acquire this ability in a couple of days, but not immediately after having their sight restored.

As it has been repeatedly emphasized, this should be taken to be at best a preliminary answer to Molyneux's question. Blindness is not a monolithic phenomenon. To abuse Tolstoy's famous first line of the novel *Anna Karenina*: all vision is alike, but all blind people are blind in their own way. Lots of things need to come together for someone to perceive visually. Consequently, lots of things can go wrong. There could be problems with the retina, with the main visual pathway, with the lateral geniculate nucleus, with the early cortices, and so on. Any one of these problems would result in blindness, but very different kinds of blindness (Cattaneo and Vecchi 2011). Importantly, the visual cortices of some blind people are intact and routinely register spatial information. Not so for other blind people. But depending on the functioning of the visual cortices of blind people, we should expect very different behavior after their vision is restored. In short, as disappointing as it is, Molyneux's question does not have a uniform answer.

We have seen that tactile perception is a diverse phenomenon: it may, but it does not have to, involve active tactile exploration. But it is also diverse in a different sense: the tactile input it processes can be of very different kinds. Our skin has (at least) three kinds of receptors, which, to simplify a bit, carry information about contact, about pain, and about temperature. So far, I have only talked about tactile perception that involved the first of these. But the other two forms of tactile perception – of temperature and of pain –may have played an even more central role in the evolution of this sense modality.

Pain perception starts with the stimulation of pain receptors, commonly referred to as nociceptors. The pain signal then travels very fast to the somatosensory cortex but even before it reaches the cortex, it can trigger response actions by means of spinal reflexes. The somatosensory cortex has a distorted map of the human body, which, in terms of structure, is somewhat reminiscent of the visual cortex inasmuch as it gives a homomorphic copy of the input. So a pinprick on your left pinkie finger and another pinprick on your left pinkie finger are localized very close together in your somatosensory cortex and a pinprick on your left ring finger only a tiny bit further from the first two. The map of the human skin in the somatosensory cortex is quite distorted, though, as more area is devoted to those parts of the body that have more tactile receptors (especially more nociceptors). A famous depiction of this somatosensory map is shown in Figure 2.4.

Pain perception is deeply intertwined with other perceptual and cognitive processes as we shall see in Section 3.3. And the same is true of temperature perception, commonly referred to as thermoception. While I mention thermoception as part of tactile perception, it should be acknowledged that there may be reasons to think that thermoception itself encompasses (at least) three different forms of perception: the (outward-directed) perception of the temperature of external objects (like the bathwater), the (inward-directed) perception of the temperature of our own body parts (my feet are cold) and core temperature perception (I feel hot/feverish) (Van Westen 2022). The latter is not a form of tactile perception at all. I want to leave open the question about whether we should consider thermoception to be partly tactile, partly not tactile or maybe as another independent sense modality. The difficulties of slotting thermoception into the standard way of dividing up the senses is yet another reason to be skeptical of any neat and unproblematic division between the senses.

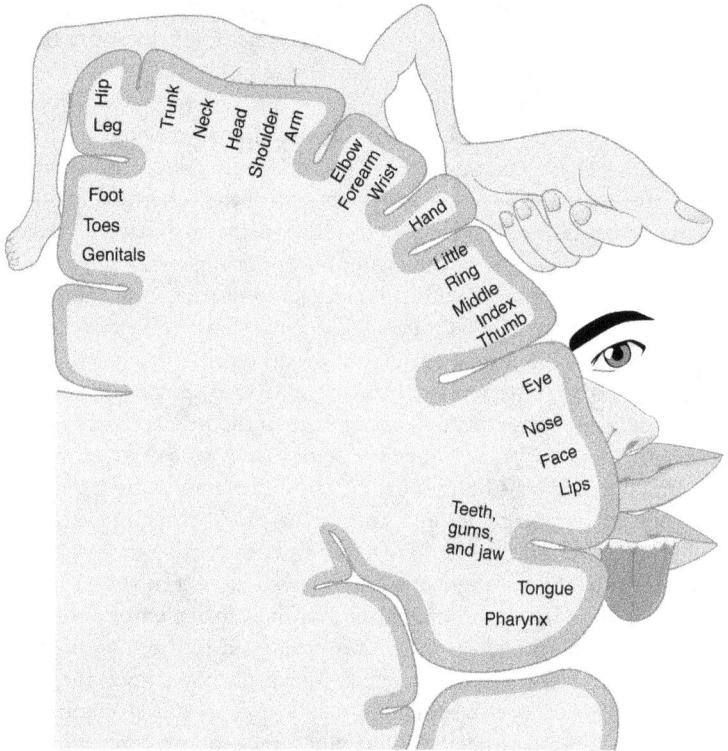

Figure 2.4 The somatosensory map in the brain (CC BY 4.0).

Another problem case is proprioception (which may include some forms of thermoception). Proprioception is the perception of one's own body (de Vignemont 2018). When you wake up in the middle of the night and you somehow sense that your left arm is under your head, this representation is proprioception. This information is not presented visually as it is dark in your room. Nor is it standard tactile perception, as your arm could also be touched by something other than the back of your head and the back of your head could also be touched by something other than your arm. I want to leave it open just what form of perception proprioception is and whether it qualifies as bona fide perception.

But the examples of thermoception and proprioception already show just how arbitrary it can be to delineate the senses. We could stuff all these diverse forms of perception into the wider bag of tactile perception, but this would paper over crucial differences between these forms of perception. And the vagueness of the division lines between different sense modalities is even more striking when it comes to the chemical senses.

2.4 THE CHEMICAL SENSES

In the traditional way of carving up the senses, we get five sense modalities: vision, audition, touch, smell, and gustatory perception. I will discuss the last two as part of one wider category as it is quite problematic to draw any kind of firm line between olfactory perception (smell) and gustatory perception (taste).

You might think that you taste food with your tongue – just as we perceive sound with our ears and we perceive colors with our eyes. But this is just wrong. Our tongue is only capable of discerning five basic tastes: sweet, sour, bitter, salty, and umami. Everything else comes from smell – from what researchers call "retronasal olfaction" (smell activated not by sniffing but by the air pushed upwards from the back of the palate). If we block smell, strawberries and mango will taste the same: sweet. Flavor perception combines input from the tongue with input from the nose. And more: heat perception and the trigeminal nerve – more on these in a minute.

The receptors in our olfactory bulb (basically the sensors in our nasal cavity, which connect your nostrils and the back of your palate) serve double duty. They get stimulated when you sniff: when you breathe in air. But they also get activated when you swallow something: the swallowing movement forces some of the air in your mouth up to your nasal cavity (see Figure 2.5). In the former case, which is called orthonasal olfaction, the hairlike endings of the olfactory receptive cells are pushed backwards and they pick up the information about the chemical composition of the air. And in the case of retronasal olfaction, the very same hairlike endings of the olfactory receptive cells are pushed forward and given that their orientation is different, they pick up different information about the chemical composition of the air. In both cases, this information is further processed in the piriform cortex, which is the first stop of olfactory processing.

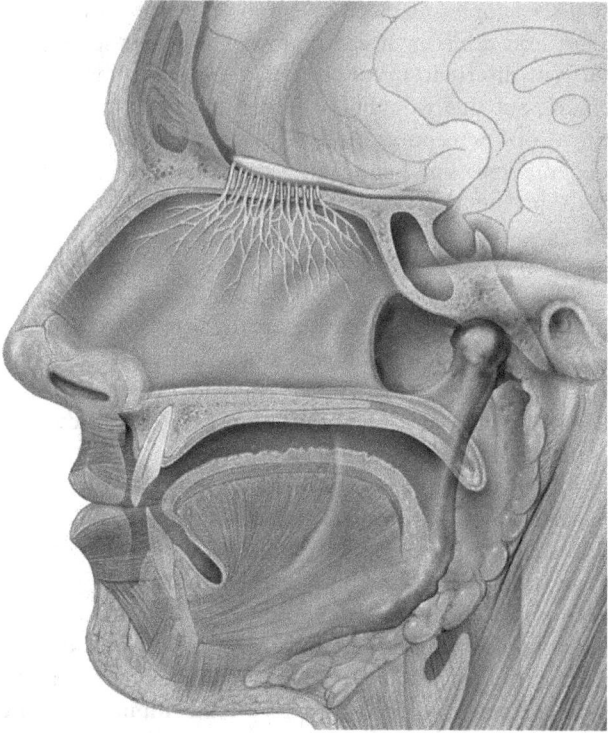

Figure 2.5 Olfactory receptive cells in the nasal cavity (Illustration by Patrick J. Lynch, CC BY2.5).

Orthonasal and retronasal olfaction use the very same sense organ. They even use the very same olfactory receptive cells. But they serve very different purposes. Orthonasal olfaction is the sense modality of smell. And retronasal olfaction is a major contributor to the sense modality of taste.

This makes drawing any kind of strict division-line between smell and taste fairly problematic. If we really wanted to make some distinctions, we could identify the sense of smell with orthonasal olfaction and the sense of taste with the combination of retronasal olfaction and the processing of the input from the tongue. Alternatively, besides the sense of smell (orthonasal olfaction) and the sense of taste (the processing of the input from the tongue), we could posit a new, third sense modality, flavor perception, which combines various different kinds of information, retronasal olfaction, and taste. Given the arbitrariness of such division-lines, I will treat smell and taste as two aspects of one wider category of sense perception, which I call *the chemical senses*.

This is not to say that smelling, when we hold a glass of wine under our nose and sniff, and tasting, when we take a sip, roll it around our mouth and swallow it, are not very different activities. They surely are. But given the complex interactions between the sensory apparatus that makes these two actions possible, it makes more sense to discuss them as two aspects of the chemical senses.

And smelling has some extremely distinctive features. The most striking of these is sniffing. Sniffing rate is very different depending on what we are smelling. Unpleasant smells trigger quick and sharp sniffing and pleasant smells trigger slow and deep sniffing. None of this is done consciously. Importantly, depending on the sniffing rate, the chemicals in the air react with the hairlike endings of the olfactory receptive cells very differently. When the sniffing is quick and sharp, the chemicals collide with these hairlike nerve endings much more forcefully and dynamically. When the sniffing is slow, this collision is gentler. The further processing of olfactory stimulus heavily depends on this initial connection between the odorants in the air and the nerve endings. In other words, the further processing of olfactory stimulus heavily depends on how we sniff (Mainland and Sobel 2006).

To put it somewhat simplistically, sniffing is to olfaction what eye movements are to vision. As we have seen in Section 2.1, vision would not be the same without eye movements. Similarly, olfaction would not be the same without sniffing. A shared feature of these two sense modalities is that perception entails some form of activity. This is not an intentional action: not something we set out to do deliberately. But it is an activity all the same. I will say more about the ways in which perception depends on activities of this kind in Section 4.4.

Another important feature of olfaction is its rich connection to emotions. Olfaction – and by extension, flavor perception – can trigger remarkably strong emotions. This phenomenon is often discussed with reference to Marcel Proust's famous example in the first volume of *A la Recherche du Temps Perdu* of the strong emotionally laden memory triggered by the smell and flavor of the madeleine dipped into tea. While this is indeed a good example of how olfactory perception can trigger strong emotions, it should be noted that Proust gives examples of very similar experiences in each and every sense modality (not in the first, but in the last of the seven volumes, which may explain why these are overlooked.). Nonetheless, it seems that not all sense modalities are created equal when it comes to their emotional resonance.

We have seen that for humans, vision is far superior to audition. Our olfaction is even worse. This is a human-specific weakness, some other animals, for example dogs, are excellent at smelling. But our perceptual discrimination when it comes to olfaction is not very impressive. We have also seen that while audition can localize objects in space, it will be much less accurate in doing so than vision is. Olfaction is, again, even less accurate than audition. Because of this, it has been debated whether olfaction can represent spatial location at all (although one wonders whether we would have these debates if we, humans, had as good a sense of smell as dogs).

Could we localize a smelly object in space purely on the basis of olfaction? The answer here depends on how we use our noses. If you are sitting in the middle of a room, blindfolded and I put a ripe brie cheese behind you or to your left, it is close to impossible for you to tell where the cheese is. But if I let you explore the room, still blindfolded, sniffing your way around it, then you can reliably find the cheese (Porter et al. 2007).

A further odd feature of olfaction is that we can often feel odors after the source of the smell is gone. Suppose that after this experiment, I throw out the ripe brie cheese, and take out the garbage. No trace of the cheese in the room any more. But the smell can still linger. This is very different from what happens in vision, audition or tactile perception, where getting rid of the perceived object gets rid of all perception. This odd feature of olfaction plays an important role in characterizing just what it is that we smell. If we assume that we smell odors – just like we hear sounds – the question remains of how we should think about odors. And it seems that odors – unlike sounds – can completely detach from their source. The source is in the garbage truck, far away from here by now. But the odor remains (Lycan 2000).

Vision and audition bind features. When we see a red triangle, our visual system binds the property of being red and the property of being triangle-shaped together. And when we hear a loud high-pitched beep, our auditory system binds the property of being high-pitched and the property of being loud together. But does olfaction do something similar?

One way of making this question sharper is to think of two contrasting visual scenarios: a red triangle next to a green circle and a green triangle next to a red circle. These two visual scenarios are clearly different, and this difference is explained by the fact that the features are bound together differently. In one case, red and triangular are bound together, and in the other, red and circular are bound together (Jackson 1977). But how does this play out in olfaction? Take the following two olfactory scenarios. First scenario: you smell a burnt cauliflower and a piece of rotten salmon. Second scenario: you smell a rotten cauliflower and a piece of burnt salmon. Can we distinguish between these two smellscapes purely on the basis of olfaction? I am not sure. Some have argued that we can't and, as a result, olfaction does not bind features together (Batty 2010). If this is so, it would be a major difference in comparison to the visual case of the red triangle and the green circle.

So much about smelling. How about flavor perception? We have seen that flavor perception is influenced by smell. But not only that (Smith 2012). It is also influenced by thermoception, which, as we have seen, is best categorized as a subspecies of touch. One famous example of this is the influence of temperature perception on the taste of sugar. Sugary beverages taste much less sugary when they are colder – something the producers and advertisers of some major sugary beverage brands clearly know very well. So thermoception has a major influence not only on flavor but also on one of the five basic tastes that our tongue can discern: sweetness.

Another important contributor to flavor perception is the trigeminal nerve, a nerve that runs along the side of our face and that picks up on various mechanical stimuli primarily on our face, but also in our mouth. Without trigeminal nerve input, we would not be able to feel the coolness of mint, the spiciness of a papaya salad, or the astringence of pomegranate.

All these diverse forms of perceptual processing – taste perception, olfaction, thermoception, trigeminal processing – contribute to flavor perception. In this sense, flavor perception is deeply multimodal. Different sense modalities work together and their intertwined functioning results in the experience of flavor. The next section will show that flavor perception is not an exception from this point of view, but it is rather the rule. In the human perceptual system, multimodal perception is the norm.

2.5 MULTIMODAL PERCEPTION

Let's stay with the example of flavor perception a bit more. Flavor perception, as we have seen, is deeply multimodal: it is a composite of what happens on your tongue, in your nose, with your temperature receptors, among others. But the multimodality of flavor perception is even more remarkable.

Flavor perception is also influenced by sight and sound. White noise, for example, has a terrible influence on our flavor perception – that is one of the main reasons why food tends to taste awful on airplanes (Woods et al. 2011). When you put on noise-cancelling headphones, the taste improves significantly (well, depending on the airline…). And our assessment of how tasty potato chips are is heavily influenced by the sound they make when we bite on them (Spence 2015). When the auditory stimulus is manipulated in a way that amplifies the crunch it makes in your mouth, the loudness of the crunching sound the chips appear to make is a better predictor of your rating of the tastiness of the chips than any other factor.

Further, the color of the food we are eating can also have a significant influence here. The weight of a spoon influences the perceived quality of yoghurt (the heavier the spoon, the creamier the yoghurt tastes). The color of the cup influences the perceived taste of hot chocolate (for best effect, use orange mugs!). And the weight of the glass also influences the perceived quality of wine (Hummel et al. 2003). (You may want to avoid heavy wine-glasses at your next dinner party). Flavor perception is a fragile and extremely complex phenomenon: change one small thing in pretty much any sense modality and it can have a powerful (often negative) effect (Spence et al. 2014, Smith 2012).

We think we know what kind of food we like, but there are all these completely irrelevant effects on what we like and what we don't. This is one way in which we wildly overestimate our access to our own mind. You may think you are a coffee connoisseur, but your enjoyment of coffee correlates much more closely with the shape of the cup or the lighting of the room than with the actual liquid you are drinking.

But shouldn't we then conclude that we really waste our time when we go to wine-tasting events or to a fancy restaurant? The enjoyment we get out of these will depend on factors we have little or no control over. The popular media were quick to jump at these results and present them as solid scientific evidence that wine-connoisseurship is plain bullshit (their word, not mine, see, e.g., Gonzalez 2013).

One result that is widely reported at various news sites and newspapers is that even professional wine-tasters are sometimes bad at distinguishing red wine and white wine if they smell or taste them without having any information about the wine's color (either because they are drinking it from black glasses or because the white wine is colored red with tasteless colorant) (Morrot et al. 2001). While the experiment that this conclusion is based on is often misreported, one can see how you can grab headlines with this. If wine experts can't even tell red and white wine apart, what on earth do they have to pontificate about?

Even worse, these studies show that the bias from the perceived color is even stronger in wine experts than in novices like you or me (Wang and Spence 2019). So if years of culinary schooling and wine tasting lead to more confusion, what's the point? While it is tempting to frame these oddities of flavor perception as signs that our perception, and even the perception of trained experts, is extremely unreliable, this would be the wrong conclusion to draw.

Perception in general is multimodal: information from a number of sense modalities is combined when you see or hear something. This goes beyond food perception. A simple example of multimodal perception is ventriloquism, where your auditory experience is influenced by something visible (Bertelson 1999). We experience the voices as coming from the dummy, while they in fact come from the ventriloquist. The auditory sense modality identifies the ventriloquist as the source of the voices, while the visual sense modality identifies the dummy. And, as it often (not always – see O'Callaghan 2008) happens in crossmodal illusions, the visual sense modality wins out: our (auditory) experience is of the voices as coming from the dummy.

Here is another example: If there is a flash in your visual scene and you hear two beeps while the flash lasts, you experience it as two flashes (Shams et al. 2000). This is one of the few examples where seeing does not trump hearing. The two beeps we hear influence the processing of the one flash in our visual sense modality and, as a result, our visual experience is as of two flashes. From neuroimaging studies of this 'double flash illusion,' we also know that the interaction between the visual and the auditory processing in this case is extremely early, it happens in the primary sensory cortices: we can decode two flashes in the primary visual cortex – which is a result of the two beeps and not of the one flash that registers on the retina (Watkins et al. 2006).

Given this deep multimodality of our perceptual system, what we should expect when it comes to the enjoyment of food and wine is that all the sense modalities can be involved in these experiences. If taste, smell, texture perception and thermal perception are combined, why would seeing and hearing be irrelevant? We are creatures with multimodal perception. That's what we're good at. Expecting us to be good at blocking all sense modalities but one would just set us up for failure.

The interaction between the senses will play an important role throughout the book. But it also poses a challenge to the perceptual system in general. The information that different sense modalities provide would need to be somehow united. For example, if I see a flash in the top left corner of my visual field and I hear a chirping sound from somewhere above toward the left, the perceptual system binds these two pieces of input together. But what allows it to do so? How does the perceptual system know that these two pieces of input belong together? Does it have some kind of pre-existing spatial representation and it places the incoming info in this coordinate system? I will say more about this issue in Section 4.2.

I started the chapter with a discussion of just how difficult it is to individuate the senses. We have seen that some seemingly straightforward ways of doing so would not work very well. But at this point, we may wonder whether the individuation of the senses is such an important question to begin with. After all, the way human perception works is by combining and uniting the information the different senses give us and it does so at an extremely early stage of perceptual processing. We have seen in great detail in Section 1.2, just what a difficult job perception has, having to figure out the most likely model of the world on the basis of extremely sparse input. So it is hardly surprising that perception throws everything it has at the task, regardless of what sense modality the information originates from.

I discussed a variety of different sense modalities. But I also missed out on many. I restricted the discussion to senses that we, humans have. Other animals can have very different senses (see Godfrey-Smith 2020). Just one example: echolocation is a form of perception that bats, dolphins, and some species of whales are known to use. It consists of emitting sounds and given the different rates in which the thus emitted sound waves return to their ears, the animal's brain can gain information about the outline of the features around it. Echolocation is a well-studied and fairly well-understood phenomenon in bats, dolphins, and some species of whales. But humans can also echolocate, and blind people can as well, some remarkably successfully. The general technique is to emit hardly audible clicks and it is the varying rates of the echo of these clicks that provide information about the features around the subject (Dodsworth et al. 2020). I will say more about echolocation in Section 5.5.

In closing, I want to return to the question about whether wine experts are charlatans. They are very good at perceiving – that is, at multimodal perception. They are less good at restricting their judgment to one and only one sense modality. But isn't this exactly what they are supposed to do? As we shall see in Section 3.3, what they are supposed to do is to give an assessment about one sense modality in the light of their highly developed *expectations*, which take various multimodal input into consideration. The importance of perceptual expectation not just in wine experts but in perception, more generally, takes us to the question about the ways perception and post-perceptual processes interact, which is the topic of the next chapter.

2.6 SUMMARY

Perception gives us access to the world by means of a variety of sense modalities: not just by seeing (which has dominated the philosophical, psychological and neuroscientific discussion of perception), but by hearing, touching, smelling, and tasting, for example. And we should not generalize from vision to all these other sense modalities because there are significant differences between them.

Further, these sense modalities don't work independently from one another: they influence each other at the earliest possible stages of perceptual processing. As a result, multimodal perception is the norm, not the exception, which should take us even further from the exclusive focus on vision in the (philosophical, psychological, and neuroscientific) study of perception.

PERCEPTION AND COGNITION

3.1 THE PERCEPTION/COGNITION DIVIDE

If perception is the process that gets us from the input to post-perceptual processing, then in order to understand what perception is, we need to be able to delineate it both from the sensory input and from post-perceptual processing. Lots of things count as post-perceptual: our beliefs, our memories, our emotions, our desires. The post-perceptual part of processing is often referred to as *cognition*: everything that is post-perceptual is cognitive. But this is an extremely broad sense of using this term. Emotions are often taken to be different from cold cognition. Ditto for desires. The interaction between perception and post-perceptual processes, which is what this chapter is about, is in many ways as interesting and important when it comes to emotions or desires as it is in the case of beliefs (Nanay 2006, Stokes 2012). Nonetheless, in this chapter, when I use the term 'cognition,' I will primarily refer to beliefs, not desires or emotions.

So, what is the difference between perception and cognition? This is a much-discussed question in philosophy of perception (Block 2023), and we have already tackled debates that presuppose some forms of answering this question. When discussing perceptual representations in Section 1.3, we have seen that while all possible features

DOI: 10.4324/9781032639536-3

can be represented post-perceptually, only a limited range of features can be represented perceptually. And there are important debates about whether, say, dispositional properties (like being fragile) or action-properties (like being graspable) can be represented perceptually or only post-perceptually (Boghossian and Velleman 1989, Nanay 2011b, 2012b). When discussing audition in Section 2.2, we have seen that it has been debated whether speech perception really qualifies as perception or whether speech is processed post-perceptually. In short, many debates will heavily rely on drawing this perception/cognition boundary one way or another.

I have been framing this question as if there were some strict border between perception and cognition: a precise point, where perception stops and cognition begins. But there are two ways of questioning this assumption, one more radical than the other.

The radical one would just deny that there would be any difference between perception and cognition. And if there is no difference, then there is no meaningful boundary between perceptual and post-perceptual processing. So the sensory input gets processed and earlier stages of this processing would be better described as perception, whereas later stages would be better described as cognition, but there is no substantial difference between these stages (Lupyan 2015).

A less radical way of questioning some kind of watertight perception/cognition boundary would be to allow for differences between perception and cognition, but insist that the transition from perception to cognition is a gradual one. We can acknowledge some form of continuity between perception and cognition and deny that there would be watertight division-lines in the human mind, while still insisting that there is a substantial difference between perception and cognition. The question is then: what is this substantial difference?

One way of formulating this substantial difference, while allowing for the gradual transition between perception and cognition would be to focus on the role of the sensory input itself in these various stages of processing (Beck 2018, Phillips 2019). In earlier stages, the input carries more weight than in later stages, which are more and more decoupled from the input. A potential problem with placing too much emphasis on the role of the input is that, as we shall see in Chapter 5, even the earliest stages of perceptual processing can happen without any sensory input.

But here is another way of contrasting perception and cognition, which is more promising: this substantial difference has to do with the ways in which perception and cognition represent. We have seen in Section 1.3 that the emphasis on perceptual representations helps us with delineating perception (the enriching of the sensory input) from sensory input proper: the former is representational, the latter is not. But how about the other delineating task: to keep apart perceptual from post-perceptual processing? The concept of representation can help here as well, but some more work is needed.

In Section 1.3, I introduced the concept of representation with two somewhat trivial examples: the word 'apple' and the picture of an apple. Both represent an apple. But they represent it very differently. They represent it using different formats. The word 'apple' represents using a linguistic format, whereas the picture uses an imagistic format. In the case of the photograph of the apple, there is some form of spatial correspondence between the shape of the apple and the shape on the photograph. These do not need to be the very same shape, but there needs to be some form of (maybe partial) spatial correspondence. There is no spatial correspondence between the shape of the apple and any feature of the word 'apple' whatsoever.

If I have a belief that the apple in front of me is round, the format of this belief is language-like in the sense that this belief represents in the same way as a sentence (the sentence that the apple in front of me is round) represents. But if I have a perceptual representation of the apple in front of me as round, the format of this perceptual representation is very different. It does not represent the way a sentence does. It represents in a way that is more similar to the way pictures represent (Kulvicki 2014).

This is especially clear when it comes to early cortical sensory representations, like the representations in our primary or secondary visual cortices, because these representations are retinotopic – they are homomorphic with our retina. If a triangle is projected on your retina, there will be a roughly triangle-shaped activation in the direction-sensitive neurons of your primary visual cortex. The two triangles may not be exactly the same: if the retinal triangle is incomplete, for example, the triangle could be completed in the primary visual cortex. But there is a very clear and easy way to detect spatial correspondence between the shape properties of the represented object and the shape properties represented in the primary visual cortex. There is no such spatial correspondence when it comes to beliefs.

This is a major difference between perceptual and cognitive representations. The format of perceptual representation is imagistic. The format of cognitive representation is propositional: they represent in a propositional format.

Can these ways of representing be combined? On the face of it, they can. Some maps, for example, represent in a way that is imagistic in terms of its general structure – there is a clear spatial correspondence between the map and the represented terrain. But as long as it is the kind of map that we actually use, there are also legends – symbols for, say, pharmacies, mountain peaks or villages. And there may also be labels for cities, lakes or streets. None of these represent imagistically. So maps would provide an example of what a mixed imagistic/propositional representation would look like (Camp 2007).

But are there such mixed imagistic/propositional representations in the human mind? If there are, we can do justice to the gradual transition between perception and cognition while acknowledging the substantial difference between imagistic perceptual representations and propositional cognitive representations (Quilty-Dunn 2020). In fact, it could be argued that many of the allegedly propositional mental states, for example, desires, represent at least in part imagistically (and not exclusively propositionally). The same argument could also apply to the most stereotypic of all propositional representations: beliefs. This is a book about perception, so I don't want to get into the debates about the format and content of all these non-perceptual states. But if it is true that many of these non-perceptual states represent at least in part imagistically, this gives us all the more reason to pay close attention to the way perception represents: imagistically.

3.2 TOP-DOWN INFLUENCES ON PERCEPTION

Perception is supposed to give us a reliable representation of how the world is. It is supposed to be an unbiased point of contact with the world, which is supposed to be the basis of any kind of further correct representation that relies on it.

But is perception unbiased? Parmesan cheese is very different from vomit. And they don't *really* smell the same either. But their smell is similar enough so that if you are presented with a nontransparent box full of parmesan cheese but you are told that it is vomit, you will in fact smell vomit (and the other way around, see Manescu et al. 2014). What you know (or seem to know) influences what you smell.

We have seen that perception is the processing of sensory input. This may sound like in perceptual processing information flows in one direction and one direction only: from the input upwards to the perceptual representation. In other words, it may sound like saying that perception is fully bottom-up. If perception were fully bottom-up, this would mean that it is also unbiased in some sense: it is the innocent processing of the sensory input, so no extra information is put in by the perceptual processing itself that would bias the perception (Fodor 1983, Pylyshyn 1999, Firestone and Scholl 2016, see also Orlandi 2014).

Again, this is one tempting way of thinking about perception. And it is tempting partly because it seems that the alternative is wrought with problematic consequences. The alternative is that perception would somehow be biased by our pre-existing representations of the world. So it is not fully bottom-up driven. It is susceptible to top-down influences. This picture of perception, on the face of it, has extremely problematic consequences as this would mean that we can't use perception as an unbiased source of information. To put it very simply, if perception depends on what we know, it can't be a very good source of knowledge. We would get a form of vicious circularity: perception depends on our beliefs and our beliefs depend on perception. This is not exactly a recipe for learning about how the world is (as opposed to how we already think the world is).

While the picture of fully bottom-up perceptual processing, which provides unbiased information to the post-perceptual parts of the mind, is attractive inasmuch as it solves the vicious circularity I talked about in the previous paragraph, it is also remarkably false.

Take the primary visual cortex again, the first stop in visual processing. If the bottom-up picture of perceptual processing were correct, this would mean that information from the retinal input is transmitted to the primary visual cortex, which, in isolation from the rest of the brain, processes this input and outputs some kind of representation for further processing.

This is blatantly not what happens in the primary visual cortex. In a remarkable set of studies it was discovered that only 5%–10% of the incoming signal to the primary visual cortex comes from the retina. The rest comes laterally (from other parts of the primary visual cortex) or from top-down sources (Douglas and Martin 2007). In other words, top-down influences on perceptual processing are rampant.

We have also seen in Section 1.4 that the processing in the primary visual cortex is extremely sensitive to the allocation of attention as well as to lateral influences from other sense modalities. The fully bottom-up picture of perception is factually incorrect. Perceptual processing is not a one-way street. Information flows in both directions.

Take two of the illustrations used in earlier chapters: the Kanizsa triangle and the dolphin picture (Figures 2.1 and 2.2a, b). We now know that the processing of the illusory contours of the Kanizsa triangle in the primary visual cortex is triggered by the representation of these contours in the secondary visual cortex (Qiu and von der Heydt 2005). So it is a top-down influence from the secondary to the primary visual cortex.

The same goes for the image with the dolphin. When you look at Figure 2.2a for the first time, the direction-sensitive neurons in the primary visual cortex that corresponds to the dolphin's eye, for example, are silent. After all they are in the middle of a homogenous black region. But after seeing Figure 2.2b, they are extremely active. So processing in the primary visual cortex is sensitive to something that is clearly not bottom-up. In the Kanizsa triangle example, it is clearly understood where these top-down influences on the primary visual cortex come from: from the secondary visual cortex. In the case of the dolphin image, it is less clear, but wherever they originate from, it must be further up from the primary visual cortex.

These are just two examples, but the interaction between bottom-up and top-down processes is the norm in perception. Perceptual processing is often influenced in a top-down manner by higher-level mental states and processes (see Vetter and Newen 2014, Teufel and Nanay 2017 for a summary).

I talked about the perception-cognition divide in Section 3.1. One important question is whether there are top-down influences that cross this divide. Remember that the main motivation for taking top-down influences on perception to be a bad thing is that if perception is influenced by cognition, then it can't be an unbiased basis for cognition.

The results about the two-way interactions between, say, the primary and the secondary visual cortex don't show that cognition influences perception – it shows that higher stages of perceptual processing influence lower stages of perceptual processing. But on the basis of what we know about the brain, it would be very unlikely to posit some kind of watertight and heavily patrolled barricade between perception (where top-down influences are rife) and cognition. Earlier stages of perceptual processing (say, in the primary visual cortex) are influenced by later stages (say, the secondary visual cortex), and these later stages are influenced by even later stages and those by lower ranks of cognitive processing, and so on.

Where does this leave us with regard to the circularity worry, that is, the unbiased nature of perception? If cognitive processes influence perception, then perception can't be taken to be an unbiased guide to how the world is. We always see the world through the veil of the prejudices our beliefs and other cognitive processes provide.

Is this really a worry? Remember what the perceptual system is supposed to do. It has the incredibly difficult task of putting together a representation of the features of the world around us on the basis of very sparse input that we receive through the senses. If the perceptual system is to come up with the most likely model of the world around us, it is better off using all kinds of information that it has about the likely layouts and the most probable arrangements of features. And this very much includes information that is stored outside the perceptual system.

In other words, the fact that perception is not unbiased is not necessarily a bad thing. Paradoxically, if it is biased, it could give us a more accurate representation of the world around us. And the best demonstration of this is perceptual learning (I want to leave open the question about whether perceptual learning counts as top-down influence – the point is that the bias it introduces is not a negative influence).

As we have seen in Section 1.4, perceptual learning is the psychological phenomenon that perceiving a certain kind of stimulus leaves a mark on the perceptual system, so the next time you perceive a similar kind of stimulus, your perception of it will be different.

Because of perceptual learning, our perception depends on past perceptual episodes – on what kind of perceptual stimuli we've encountered before. Our imprinted perceptual history (dictated by what we have encountered throughout our lives and especially in our early formative years) has an impact on how we perceive the world now.

Perception is not a fixed mechanism. It changes over our lifetime. What you perceive now influences how you perceive the world later. In some cases, this influence can be quite radical. Consider the example of perceptual discrimination (see Stokes and Nanay 2020). Fingerprint experts can differentiate two very similar fingerprints quickly and reliably – in a way novices cannot. Before undergoing extensive forensic fingerprint training, the expert looked at the very same stimulus she does now, but her perceptual processes and her perceptual experience are very different. We know from a number of empirical studies that this change entails a change in the way her perceptual system works (see Busey and Parada 2010, Jarodzka et al. 2010).

The effects of perceptual learning are the most impressive when it comes to perceptual expertise, like in the fingerprint example (or in the case of expert radiologists, who can, above chance, identify an anomaly in a radiographic image in 200 ms (Evans et al. 2013)). But perceptual learning is not limited to these examples (see Stokes 2021). What you see and how you see is not determined by the object and its properties (and the illumination conditions). It depends heavily on your perceptual history.

But in many cases of perceptual learning, for example, in the cases of expertise, the impact of perceptual learning is clearly positive: it helps us to have a more accurate representation of, say, the fingerprints or the anomaly in the radiographic images. If perception relied only on unbiased processing, we would have a much less accurate representation of the world around us.

3.3 PERCEPTUAL EXPECTATIONS

One really important category of top-down influences on perception is perceptual expectations. Perception would not be what it is without perceptual expectations. Now, expectations come in various flavors. I could have an expectation that my dentist's visit that is scheduled for next week is going to be unpleasant. Or I could have an expectation that in the next James Bond film, the hero will not die at the end – a reasonable expectation in the light of 24 James Bond films from 1962 till 2015. These expectations have little to do with perception. I have some kind of non-perceptual representation about my dentist's visit next week and about the ending of the next Bond flick.

But not all expectations are like this. Some expectations are genuinely perceptual. My favorite example concerns escalators or moving walkways. When you step on an escalator or a moving walkway that is out of order and is not moving, you have a visceral feeling of walking way too slowly – more slowly than you would if you just continued next to the escalator on the regular stairs. What is interesting in this example is that it involves a crossmodal effect (see Section 2.5): your vision makes you expect a different speed than what you actually experience.

But expectations are extremely important in all sense modalities. For example, they play a crucial role in our engagement with music: when we are listening to a song, even if we hear it for the first time, we have some expectations of how it will continue. And when it is a tune we know, this expectation can be quite strong (and easy to study experimentally). When we hear Ta-Ta-Ta at the beginning of Beethoven's Fifth Symphony, we will strongly anticipate the closing Taaam of the Ta-Ta-Ta-Taaaam (Meyer 1956, Judge and Nanay 2021).

Much of our expectations are fairly indeterminate: when we are listening to a musical piece we have never heard before, we will have some expectations of how a tune will continue, but we do not know exactly what will happen. Our expectations are malleable and dynamic: they change as we listen to the piece.

Our expectations may also turn out to be incorrect. This is true of the non-perceptual expectations, for example, about the ending of the 25th James Bond film (apologies if I have spoiled anything…) or the painfulness of the dentist's visit. But it is also true of perceptual expectations: they can be frustrated, and expectations are the most easily recognized when they are frustrated. In the case of the escalator example, for example, our perceptual expectation about how it will feel to ride the escalator is thwarted.

It is a hotly debated question in contemporary perceptual psychology how expectation and input are weighed against one another. We have seen that it is not all input – expectations also play a role. And presumably it's not expectations only either – the input does make at least some difference. But it is not entirely clear just how much expectations and input contribute.

According to some, perception is almost all expectations: the brain is a predicting device, and our perceptual system does its best to predict what kind of input will hit our sense organs. If the prediction is wrong, it will adjust the predicting mechanisms – the expectations (Friston 2010, Hohwy 2013). In this picture, almost all the work is done by expectations and input has only a secondary role to play as the occasional adjustor of the expectations. According to other accounts, while expectation plays a key role, it does not mean that input is only secondary. Without going more deeply into these debates, it is important to stress that one point of agreement is that perceptual processing is based on the interaction between input and expectations.

One especially well-researched form of expectations involves pain perception. Pain depends on your expectations: if you are expecting pain, say, burning pain at the back of your neck (because the cruel experimenter just announced that this is what will happen), you will experience an actual painful sensation when she touches the back of your neck with an ice cube. More generally, our expectations about the pain stimulus influence pain intensity as well as pain location and even the presence of pain (Ploghaus et al. 2003, Carlino et al. 2014, see also Peerdeman et al. 2016 for a summary).

Another important example comes from adaptation illusions. Here is a very simple experiment you can do in your bathroom. Put your left hand in a bowl of cold water and put your right hand in a bowl of very warm water. Wait for a couple of minutes. Now put both hands in a third bowl, which has lukewarm water. The same bowl of (lukewarm) water will feel very hot for your left hand and it will feel very cold for your right hand (see Tritsch 1990 – the phenomenon was described already in John Locke's *Essay Concerning Human Understanding* (1690, 2.8.21). It's quite a disconcerting experience.

This is an example of an adaptation illusion. Our perceptual system is susceptible to short-term adaptations. This is a form of perceptual change, but it is different from perceptual learning inasmuch as its time scale is much shorter, usually just a couple of minutes and in that it does not leave a permanent mark on how you will perceive things in the distant future.

What is interesting about adaptation illusions is that the perceptual system forms something like a short-term expectation on the basis of recent input and this short-term expectation influences our perception. But these short-term expectations can go straight against our beliefs and more high-level expectations. For example, we all have fairly firm expectations that the same bowl of water should have the same temperature, regardless of which hand you're dipping in it. This is a higher-level, let's say, cognitive expectation. But the lower-level perceptual expectations provided by the heat adaptation of your left hand and the very different lower-level perceptual expectations provided by the heat adaptation of your right hand go straight against this cognitive expectation.

Expectations are about the future. We have seen that one difference between perceptual adaptation and perceptual learning concerns their time-scale. But appreciating the importance of expectations can help us to navigate an old and important aspect of perception, namely, its connection to time.

On the face of it, there is something deeply puzzling about the relation between perception and time. When we perceive an event, we do not merely perceive one snapshot after another. Perception is a temporally unfolding process and it has a certain temporal thickness: in every second, our perceptual state encompasses more than just that moment. This general idea was much talked about at the birth of what is now known as perceptual psychology, with William James famously referring to this phenomenon as 'specious present,' which he describes as "no knife–edge, but a saddle–back, with a certain breadth of its own" (James 1890, p. 609, see also Phillips 2011).

But if this is correct, then we perceptually represent not only the present moment, but also what has just happened as well as what is about to happen. This is easier to swallow when it comes to what has just happened as the perceptual memory-traces of the very recent past are still present in the perceptual system. But how can we perceive something that has not happened yet? After all, isn't perception supposed to be a causal concept? And the cause always comes before the effect. Then how can something that will only happen in the future cause my current perceptual state?

The answer is that we do not strictly speaking perceive the future. That would be odd. Rather, we have expectations about the future and our perceptual state is the mixture of (causally triggered) input about the current state of affairs and expectations about the near future.

The importance of expectations will also help us to put to bed the worries from Section 2.5 about the competence of wine experts. To recap, we are all pretty bad at distinguishing red wine and white wine if we only smell or taste them without having any information about the wine's color. As we have seen, in one widely publicized finding, experts were even more prone to be misled in experiments of this kind. They tasted white wines, which were colored red with tasteless colorant. And many of them never noticed that it was white wine and gave (mistaken) characterization of the wine they thought to be red.

We can frame these results as the definitive verdict that wine experts are charlatans. But there is a much simpler explanation. Experts have way more, and more precise, top-down expectations than novices: They have spent years developing exactly these expectations. This is very clear in the case of the fingerprint and radiology examples we considered in Section 3.2. And it is also true of wine experts. So in unusual scenarios when they are misled (by artificial coloring), they rely on their expectations more than novices do. Novices may lack any specific expectations about the odor of wine on the basis of its color. But experts do have expectations of this kind and this will influence their judgment.

In other words, the wine expert is not doing anything wrong. Given what she sees, she is expecting what she should be expecting. But she is being tricked. The liquid in her glass has features that no wine should have. It's white wine that looks red.

3.4 CROSS-CULTURAL DIFFERENCES

There are many things about perception that are universal. Regardless of what part of the world you grew up in, your retinal input is transferred to the primary visual cortex. But not everything about perception is universal and the top-down influences on perception can help us explain these cross-cultural differences. Very briefly, as perception is influenced in a top-down manner and as the higher-level mental states differ across cultures, perception also differs across cultures.

A good entry point for the discussion of cross-cultural differences in perception comes from studies on attention. In the last two decades or so, more and more studies have been published about the differences in the way East Asians and Westerners exercise their visual attention. The general line of argument is that while Westerners attend more to focal objects, East Asians are more likely to attend to the background context. For example, when looking at short footage of an aquarium, Westerners tend to attend to the moving fish, whereas East Asians tend to attend to features such as the bubbles and the seaweed (Masuda and Nisbett 2001). As we have seen in Section 1.4, perception heavily depends on where we focus our attention. Hence, we get a cross-cultural difference in attention and also in perception.

Other studies show that Westerners and East Asians behave differently in change blindness experiments (Masuda and Nisbett 2006). Change blindness experiments are somewhat similar to inattentional blindness experiments (like the one about the invisible gorilla) inasmuch as they show that we fail to experience those aspects of the visual scene that we are not attending to. But this is achieved, in the case of change blindness experiments, by means of changing some relatively minor (although sometimes not so minor) features of the scene. This can take various forms, probably the most striking one is when during a film clip, some feature of the scene is changed very slowly. But it also works if the subjects are presented with two images (sometimes with a mask presented briefly between them). The subject fails to notice these changes, although they can be very significant indeed. The importance of the change blindness experiments in the present context is that Americans detect more changes occurring in the features of the focal objects, whereas Japanese subjects detect more changes occurring in the background.

There are many other experiments that point in the same direction. Eye-tracking studies suggest that American subjects focus longer (and sooner) on focal objects, whereas East Asians are more likely to focus away from the focal objects (Chua et al. 2005). And East Asians

are much worse at the 'rod and frame' task than Americans, an experimental setup, where subjects have to determine the orientation of a
line that is framed in a rectangle. If the alignment of the line and the
framing rectangle is not the same, all subjects experience an optical
illusion with regard to the orientation of the line, but East Asians
experience a higher degree of discrepancy in the alignment of the
line and the frame. And this is often explained with reference to their
more holistic way of looking at visual scenes (Ji et al. 2000). Finally,
East Asians seem to be better at attending to, encoding, and remembering relations between elements of a scene than Westerners who
are better at attending to, encoding, and remembering the features of
the elements themselves (Goh et al. 2007).

These studies are often embedded in some larger scale conjectures
about attitudinal differences between cultures—maybe Americans or
Westerners in general are more individualist, whereas East Asian cultures are less individualistic and more communal (see Markus and
Kitayama 1991, Nisbett et al. 2001, Nisbett 2003, Boduroglu et al.
2009 for good overviews). These wider assumptions about large-scale
cultural differences are controversial (and caused some media frenzy),
but they are irrelevant from the point of view of this book. What is
important is that there seems to be a well-documented difference
in the way East Asians and Westerners exercise their attention. The
reasons for these differences are cultural: they have to do with the
way the subjects have been socialized (just what aspect of socialization makes the difference—the complexity of visual scenes routinely
encountered, the differences in reading, etc.—is an open question,
see Miyamoto et al. 2006).

I have been focusing on the cross-cultural variations in perceptual
attention because this is an especially thoroughly studied phenomenon. But there is a wider point here. Take perceptual learning again.
We have seen that our perception now is heavily dependent on our
perceptual history. But someone who grew up in rural South-East
Tanzania has a very different perceptual history from someone who
grew up in downtown San Francisco. Given the cross-cultural variations in perceptual history, there will be cross-cultural variations in
perception per se.

Further, if perception is influenced in a top-down manner by our
other mental states, for example, background beliefs, then people

with different background beliefs will have different perceptual states. And then given that people who grew up in different parts of the world may have very different background beliefs, they will, because of the top-down influences on perception, perceive the world very differently.

Just how far up do the top-down influences that are responsible for these cross-cultural variations come from is a question I want to leave open. In some cases, these top-down influences may not come from very high up – definitely not from beliefs. But there may be reasons to think that top-down influences on perception can also come from as high up as it gets: language.

The relation between perception and language is a complicated one. One issue that I have mentioned in Section 3.1 is the difference in the format of perceptual and linguistic representations. Another issue is about the ways in which perception influences language, something usually discussed under the heading of concept acquisition. But what I want to focus on now is the question about how language influences perception.

An old and influential thought in the history of philosophy, psychology, and linguistics is that the language you speak influences the way you see the world. Different languages segment the color space differently. Russian, for example, has two different words for what we call 'blue,' roughly corresponding to light blue and dark blue. Does this imply that they perceive the world differently? Some findings suggest so: native Russian speakers see two shades of blue that saddle the divide between light blue and dark blue as more different than English native speakers (Winawer et al. 2007, Maier and Rahman 2018). If the language we speak influences the way we see the world, then this is a major source of cross-cultural variations in perception.

The effects of the light blue vs. dark blue categorization on our perception are relatively minor. But there are more extreme examples. Speakers of the Kuuk Thaayorre language in the aboriginal Pormpuraaw people who live in Queensland, Australia, for example, perceive space and time very differently from the way we do. First, they represent the space around them geographically. So instead of saying that something is on their left, they say, something is to the West. But things get even more interesting when it comes to the representation of time.

Most of us think of time as flowing from left to right or from right to left (evidenced, for example, by the way graphs about timelines are arranged), and this may have something to do with the direction in which we read. One reason to think so is that Arabic and Hebrew speakers tend to represent time as flowing from right to left. An interesting exception to this rule comes from the studies of Aymara speakers, who live in the Andes in South America (Núñez and Sweetser 2006). They represent time as flowing from front to back. So the past is ahead of us, whereas the future is behind us. While this contrasts with some of the metaphors we English-speakers use (as we talk about the future being ahead of us), it could also be said to be more in line with how we actually experience time (as we only have access to what has already happened).

The Kuuk Thaayorre speakers represent time as flowing from east to west (Boroditsky and Gaby 2010). So depending on whether they are facing north or south, they represent time as flowing right to left or left to right, respectively. When they see a landscape, regardless of which direction they are facing, they will represent the past in the east and the future in the west. Now, strictly speaking, these findings are about the representation of time, not of perception proper. But if a Kuuk Thaayorre speaker is looking at a landscape and you are looking at the very same landscape, the two perceptual states will be very different as the perceptual states of the Kuuk Thaayorre speaker – but not yours – will be heavily infused with the representation of past and future.

These well-demonstrated cross-cultural differences in perception have serious consequences when it comes to the methodology of studying perception. We have already discussed a number of problems with using introspection to find out about perception in Section 1.3. But given the cross-cultural differences in perception, we have an even stronger reason to avoid all kinds of appeals to introspective evidence of (invariably Western) thinkers when it comes to the study of perception.

Even if introspection were 100% reliable (and we have seen that it isn't) and thus it gave us full access to the nature and content of our own perceptual state, this would only give us full access to the nature and content of the perceptual state of one individual only, who grew up in a very specific cultural milieu and thus has a very specific perceptual history. This introspective evidence would not give us much guidance (and definitely not 100% reliable guidance) to how other people who grew up in a different cultural milieu and thus have a very different perceptual history see the world. In short, because of the cross-cultural variations in perception, we should avoid, at all costs, generalizing from our own introspective evidence.

Again, the way the rods and cones fire in our retina may be universal and the same in all humans. Edge segmentation in the early visual cortices also works the same way. But the further up we go in the visual hierarchy, the more space there is for top-down influences on perception and, as a result, more space for cross-cultural variability.

3.5 PERCEPTUAL JUSTIFICATION

This chapter has been mainly about top-down influences on perception. And I have been assuming throughout that these top-down influences supplement the bottom-up processing of the sensory input. But the bottom-up processing of the sensory input plays an important role in understanding how perception leads to cognition.

We have seen that this is one of the two crucial functions that perception fulfills. Besides guiding action, perception also has the function of leading to correct non-perceptual representations (or beliefs). To put it very simply, perception can, and often does, yield knowledge.

You are looking at a red apple and this perceptual state gives rise to the belief that there is a red apple in front of you. This is a pretty straightforward transition from the perceptual state and the belief as they both represent a very similar state of affairs: a red apple in front of you. But the transition is not always this straightforward: if you arrive home and smell freshly made coffee, this could yield the belief that your partner has arrived before you did and has made coffee. In this case, the perceptual state and the belief it gives rise to represent very different states of affairs.

But even in those cases – like in the case of seeing the red apple – where the perceptual state and the belief represent the same things, as we have seen in Section 3.1, the format of these two kinds of representations is still very different. So the transition from a perceptual state to a belief is never simple (Helton and Nanay 2023).

I have been using terms like *the perceptual state leads to*, or *yields*, or *gives rise to*, beliefs. These are causal concepts: first you have a perceptual state and then this perceptual state causes you to have a belief. But the transition from the perceptual state to the belief is not merely causal. It can also be a form of justification. The perceptual state does not merely cause the belief, it also justifies the belief – this is why perception can ground knowledge.

The concept of justification and the concept of knowledge are central concepts of the philosophical discipline of epistemology (Lyons 2009). And perception has been an important subject of epistemological inquiry because most of what we know we know on the basis of perception. It is important to stress that not everything we know is based on perception. Many things we know from testimony (Lackey 2006). We know many things because someone else, whom we trust, told us so. When I read the weather forecast on my computer and form a belief that it is raining outside, this belief is formed on the basis of testimony (I ignore for a moment that reading the weather forecast on my computer screen entails having a perceptual state). So not all of our knowledge is based on perception. But a lot of it is.

Another way of capturing the same point is to say that perception can justify our beliefs. It can give us reason to be confident that the belief is true. And in epistemology, there are many accounts of what perceptual justification amounts to. I will keep a safe distance from these debates, but in the context of this book, it is important to note that these debates about the nature of justification in epistemology heavily depend on the stance we take on issues that are strictly about perception.

Take unconscious perception as an example. As we have seen, there is overwhelming evidence that perception can be unconscious. But depending on one's epistemological approach, there may or may not be a difference between conscious and unconscious perception when it comes to epistemic force. According to many (albeit not all) accounts in epistemology, unconscious perceptual states are just as capable of justifying our beliefs as conscious ones. For example, if perceptual justification is merely a matter of reliability, that is, if a belief is justified by a perceptual state if it is reliably caused by this perceptual state, then, given that unconscious perceptual states are just as capable of reliably causing beliefs as conscious ones, unconscious perceptual states can also play a justificatory role (Goldman 1999). According to some other accounts, perception needs to be conscious in order for it to justify anything as justification has to do not with reliability, but with providing (conscious) reasons (Pryor 2000). Again, for the purposes of this book, the details of these debates are not so relevant. What is important is that doing epistemology in some very real sense requires us to be clear about some of the key concepts and debates about perception (Berger et al. 2018).

I said that epistemologists are interested in perception because, to use the phrase this book started with once again, perception is our window to the world. Perception plays a much more interesting and central role in our mental apparatus than just fulfilling a purely epistemic function. It does lots of things that have nothing to do with anything epistemic. For example, it plays a crucial role in the guiding and monitoring of actions, which is the subject I now turn to.

3.6 SUMMARY

There was a time in the distant past when philosophers, and even some psychologists, believed that while perception can influence cognition, cognition can't influence perception – and that is a good thing, otherwise we would get a vicious circularity where we see what we believe. Now we know that this is not so – there are numerous top-down influences on already the earliest stages of perceptual processing. Just where (and how far up) these top-down influences come from is, however, debated. The differences in these top-down influences on perception help us to explain the cross-cultural differences in the way we perceive.

But perception also influences our cognition – in fact, it can and often does lead to knowledge. You look out of the window, see that it is raining outside and form a belief that it is raining outside. Sometimes (in fact, very often), this belief is justified. If so, we talk about perceptual justification. But it is unclear what this justification entails: whether perception automatically leads to (prima facie) perceptual justification or if there is a gap between perception and knowledge.

PERCEPTION AND ACTION

4.1 HOW PERCEPTION LEADS TO ACTION

You are looking at an apple, something happens in your head and then you reach out and grab the apple. What is this something that happens in your head? In some sense, this is the most basic question we can ask about the mind. After all, when we observe someone – be that a subject in a psychological experiment or our best friend – the only things we have access to are what they perceive and how they act. The rest, to be a bit dramatic, is mystery.

I lumped together subjects in a psychological experiment and your best friend in the previous paragraph for a reason. When you are trying to figure out why your best friend doesn't order steak tartare, although you know that this is her favorite in this restaurant, the way you try to make sense of this is by attributing beliefs and desires to her. You may think that she had a steak tartare for lunch and didn't want to order the same thing twice. Or you may think she is pregnant, she believes that raw beef is dangerous for pregnant women and she does not want to risk it. All of these explanations are explanations in terms of beliefs and desires.

Luckily enough, if it is your best friend whose action you're trying to figure out, you can just ask her. And her answer will probably also

DOI: 10.4324/9781032639536-4

appeal to beliefs and desires. We routinely attribute beliefs and desires not only to our friends, but also to strangers we have never seen before in order to explain their behavior. And we often also attribute beliefs and desires to ourselves. Why did I come to this café today? I must have thought that the alternatives would be too crowded at this hour, and I did not want to fight for seats. An explanation in terms of beliefs and desires.

Explanations of behavior in terms of beliefs and desires are often referred to as 'folk-psychology.' It is the naïve psychologizing of the folk. It helps us get by in our daily life. Does this mean that folk psychological categories like beliefs and desires are the actual building blocks of the mind? And are they good candidates for the mental states that mediate between perception and action? Not at all.

Folk psychology is not psychology. Just as folk biology is not biology. When I take a walk in a nearby forest, it may be helpful for the purposes of finding my way around or of talking to my friends to use folk biological concepts. Not even just very naïve concepts like trees, but more precise categories like lilies, beech trees, and so on.

As it turns out, neither the word 'lily' nor the word 'beech tree' pick out scientifically respectable categories (Dupré 1981, p. 74, pp. 71–72, respectively). As John Dupré summarizes, "it is far from universally the case that the preanalytic extension of a term of ordinary language corresponds to any recognized biological taxon" (Dupré 1981, p. 73). We can understand each other very well when we talk about lilies or beech trees, but if we want to study biology, these concepts are not very helpful. Folk biology is not all wrong. It makes some (approximately) true claims, which can, in some select circumstances, help us to navigate our biological environment. But we want more than this from a scientific theory. Folk biology is not a scientific theory.

And we can run the very same argument about folk psychology. Beliefs and desires are helpful tools to make sense of people's behavior. But nobody should infer from this that the basic building blocks of the mind are beliefs and desires, just like nobody should infer from the fact that we can navigate the forest with the help of our concepts like lily and beech trees that these concepts pick out the basic building blocks of biology. Like folk biology, folk psychology is not a scientific theory either.

It is important to see that this line of argument against taking beliefs and desires to be the building blocks of the mind does not need to lead to eliminativism or reductivism – to rejecting or censoring the use of these concepts. A popular way of countering folk psychology is to urge to get rid of all talk of mental states and refer to brain states only (Churchland 1981, 1988 – also Stich 1983 although Stich changed his mind about this, see Stich 1996). I hope it is clear that it does not follow from the mistrust of concepts like 'belief' or 'desire' that we should mistrust all non-neural ways of describing the mind. The analogy from the domain of biology would be to stretch the inadequacy of concepts like 'lily' or 'beech tree' to a mistrust of all concepts except cellular level ones (or maybe chemical or microphysical ones). This is not what biologists do: they identify the biological taxa that pick out biologically explanatory groupings of plants and trees. Just because 'lily' does not pick out such a grouping, it does not follow that no concepts of the same level of description do so. In fact, the genus *Erythronium* does delineate an explanatorily very relevant kind that is widely used in plant biology. But the concept of 'lily' does not.

Similarly, just because the concept of 'belief' or of 'desire' may not latch onto a psychologically explanatory phenomenon, this doesn't mean that there are no psychological concepts that would pick out a psychologically explanatory phenomenon. In fact, the concept of representation is supposed to fulfill exactly this role.

Beliefs and desires, whatever they are, would count as representations, but representation is a much wider category. Importantly, representation is a technical concept and not an everyday language category. As we have seen in Section 1.3, representation attributes properties to something. And we have a great number of empirically motivated reasons to describe the mind as having representations (see Nanay 2014, 2022a, Shea 2018 for summaries). The general idea here is that whatever explanatory work the concept of belief can do, the more general concept of representation can do it better. And as we have empirically solid reasons to posit representations (but significantly less solid reasons for positing beliefs and desires), if we want to understand how the mind works, we should understand it in terms of representations (and not in terms of beliefs and desires).

Folk psychology, like folk biology is an imperfect and extremely approximate theory. It works some of the time and fails to work some of the time. The hope that fuels not only philosophy of mind, but also psychology and neuroscience, is to find a better theory to describe how the mind works.

While these questions about what we should consider to be the building blocks of the mind are very general, they are extremely important when we are trying to understand the ways in which perception leads to action.

One tempting picture about the relation between perception and action is that this relation is always mediated by beliefs and desires – by cognition. Your perceptual state gives rise to a belief and this belief, together with a desire (and maybe some background beliefs) gives rise to the intention to do something, and then this intention leads to the performance of the action.

Here is an example. You see it is raining outside, form a belief that it is raining outside, have a desire not to get wet, have a background belief that the best way not to get wet in the rain is to carry an umbrella and these beliefs and desires lead to the intention to take an umbrella, which, in turn, triggers the action of taking the umbrella. In this picture of what mediates between perception and action, strictly speaking, perception only interacts with cognition – the formation of beliefs – and it is cognition then that can, among other things, lead to action.

Is this picture correct? It may be correct for some of our highly complex actions (although even complex decision-making does not seem to involve the comparison of beliefs and desires, but rather various imaginative projects, see Nanay 2016b). But it is clearly not a very good description of the vast majority of prosaic actions we perform. Most of the time, when we tie our shoestrings, we don't go through these belief and desire steps. We see the shoestring, we tie it. Same for rushing through a crowded train station without bumping into other passengers – we are very unlikely to form beliefs about their whereabouts and desires to avoid bumping into them. As William James said:

> Whilst talking I become conscious of a pin on the floor, or of some dust on my sleeve. Without interrupting the conversation I brush away the dust or pick up the pin. I make no express resolve, but the mere perception of the object and the fleeting notion of the act seem of themselves to bring the latter about.
>
> (James 1890, p. 522)

One might object that while these introspection-based arguments may show that conscious beliefs are not involved in the performance of many actions, they don't show that unconscious beliefs are not involved either. But note that beliefs, conscious or unconscious, are just not very suitable for guiding our actions. In order to avoid bumping into fast-moving passengers at the train station, I need to represent their continually changing spatial location in a fine-grained manner. Beliefs are not very good at this. Beliefs are supposed to abstract away from the specificities represented by the perceptual representations they are based on. But it is exactly these specificities that are necessary for performing actions like tying our shoelaces or brushing our teeth.

Further, the timespan of some of our perceptually guided actions is also inconsistent with any kind of involvement of beliefs and desires. For professional baseball players, it famously takes only 125 milliseconds from the moment the light from the approaching ball hits their retina to initiate the motor movement (Toole and Fogd 2021). This is incredibly fast. On the basis of what we know about the timescale of sensory processing, it is just plainly not enough time for the brain to transfer perceptual representation to beliefs and then to use this belief in the triggering of actions.

It is important that rejecting the claim that beliefs and desires mediate between perception and action does not entail that nothing mediates between perception and action. Some kind of representations clearly do mediate. Otherwise we wouldn't know where to reach to in order to grab the left shoelace or which direction to veer in order not to bump into the teenager running in the opposite direction at full speed. But the representation that plays this role can be, and most often is, a perceptual representation.

In other words, very often no cognitive states mediate between perception and action. Perceptual processing leads to a perceptual representation and this perceptual representation itself guides the performance of the action. Cognition is, more often than not, bypassed.

4.2 ACTION-GUIDING PERCEPTION

As we have seen in Section 1.5, what matters from an evolutionary perspective is the successful performance of actions as only this confers a selective advantage. And the primary function of perception is to represent the world in a way that would lead to successful actions.

But what does it take to represent the world in a way that would lead to successful actions? What do perceptual representations need to represent in order to be useful for action execution? The representation of some properties is strictly necessary not only for executing an action, but even for trying to do so.

Suppose that you're trying to pick up a cup from the table in front of you. If you did not represent the spatial location of the cup, you would have no idea which direction you should reach out toward. If you did not represent the size of the cup, you would have no idea what grip size you should approach it with. If you did not represent the weight of the cup, you would have no idea how much force to exert when lifting it.

Let's call these properties, the representation of which is strictly necessary for the performance of the action, action-properties. To put it very simply, the representation of action-properties is necessary for the performance of actions (Jeannerod 1997, Nanay 2013).

But what are action-properties? When I represent the spatial location of the cup in order to be able to reach out toward it, I must represent it in an egocentric manner. If I represented it as being at such and such latitude and such and such longitude, this representation would not be able to guide my action. And if I represented the weight of the cup as 124 grams, this information would not be able to guide my action (not without some kind of information about how much force needs to be exerted in order to lift a 124-gram object).

More generally, these properties need to be represented in a way that could guide my actions. And for this, this representation needs to be indexed to the specificities of my own body and my bodily position. This may sound more complicated than it is: when I represent the spatial location of the cup, I need to represent it in relation to where my right hand is. Left of my right hand, just in front of my right hand, and so on. If I got up and walked to the other side of the table, the cup would still have the same absolute spatial location, but I would need to attribute a very different egocentric spatial location property in order to be able to reach out toward it.

Similarly, when I represent the size of the cup, I represent it in relation to my current grip size, which I may have to increase or decrease in order to be able to latch onto the cup's actual width. Again, the size action-property is egocentric: it is indexed to my grip size. The same goes for the representation of weight: it is egocentric, which, in this case, means that it is indexed to the strength of my hand.

In short, action-properties are egocentric properties: representing these egocentric action-properties is like representing something in a coordinate system the center of which is me myself (the term 'egocentric' has been used in a variety of ways – what I mean by it is this relatively simple dependence on the specificities of one's own body and bodily position).

Again, the representation of action-properties is necessary for the performance of actions. This is true regardless of how we think about the relation between perception and action. Even if the general belief-desire picture I argued against in Section 4.1 is correct, some mental representations would need to represent these action-properties in order for the action to have a chance at being performed successfully. If, as I argued in Section 4.1, often the only representations that are involved in the triggering of an action are perceptual representations, then this means that perception can and often does represent action-properties.

Remember the debate from Section 1.3 about the range of properties that are perceptually represented. Color and shape properties are perceptually represented, whereas the property of having been picked by Mr. Smith in an orchard in Brittany on a Tuesday is not perceptually represented. But how about action-properties? If the only representations involved in the performance of an action are perceptual representations, then action-properties must be perceptually represented.

On some level, this is not very surprising. If perception is geared toward action, then it would make sense if it represented those features of the environment that are relevant for action. And action-properties are exactly these features. This is not to say that perception only represents action-relevant features – more on this in Section 4.5. But it surely does represent action-relevant features, that is, action-properties.

This action-guiding nature of perception can also help us to explain an old and venerable question about perception, namely, about the perception of space. Here is one way of raising this question. We have seen that different sense modalities all attribute very different properties to the same perceived scene. But all this information from all these different sense modalities would need to be united somehow. They need to be bound in the same framework, which primarily means the same spatial framework.

The perceptual system binds together a flash in the top left corner of my visual field and a chirping sound from somewhere above toward the left. But how does the perceptual system know that these two pieces of input belong together? Does vision provide a coordinate system and audition latches onto that? Or the other way around? Or maybe there is some kind of pre-existing, maybe even innate sense modality–independent coordinate system that both vision and audition use? None of these options are too attractive (see Matthen 2014 for an overview of the options).

But if we take the action-guiding nature of perception seriously, then there is an obvious common denominator between the way vision represents the space around us and the way audition does so. Both the visual representation and the auditory one are potentially action-guiding. And there is only one action-space (Evans 1985). Regardless of whether our action is visually guided or auditorily guided, it is performed in the very same one and only space. So we have a spatial coordinate system, that of our action-space, which can serve as a reference frame that both vision and audition can bind properties to. The perception of space heavily depends on action-guiding perception.

4.3 PERCEPTUALLY GUIDED ACTIONS

In Section 1.5, I talked about how the fact that perception is geared toward helping us to perform actions has significant influences on the nature of perception, and, more specifically, on the way perception represents the world. So understanding the actions perception leads to and guides helps us to understand perception itself better. This chapter is about the converse claim: we can understand actions that perception leads to better if we take the perceptual guidance of actions seriously.

The first thing to note is that the vast majority of our bodily actions are perceptually guided (my focus here is bodily actions and

I set mental actions, like calculating the sum of 294 and 584 in one's head aside). Even the most complicated actions, like voting for this candidate or that candidate, in the end, can only be performed with perceptual guidance as without perceptual guidance, I would have no idea where I should put my pen to tick the box I wanted to tick.

We often perform one action by means of performing another. By ticking this box in the voting booth, I voted to change the government. By switching on the light, I scared away the burglars who were lurking around the house. And so on (Dretske 1988). But this hierarchy of actions always bottoms out in perceptually guided actions (like ticking the box or switching on the light).

I've been throwing this term, 'perceptually guided action' around in the last couple of paragraphs, and it seems clear enough what it means. A crucial characteristic of perceptually guided actions is that they change if the perceptual input changes. If I'm reaching for my cup, but you push it slightly to the right, my reaching movement will change. So in some ways, my action-performance tracks the perceptual changes.

Importantly, this can also happen unconsciously.

If the location (or some other relevant property) of the target of our reaching or grasping actions suddenly changes, the trajectory and/or velocity of our movement changes very quickly (in less than 100 milliseconds) afterward. The change in our movement is unconscious: subjects do not notice this change, and as it occurs within 100 milliseconds of the change in the target's location, there is not enough time for the information to reach consciousness (Pelisson et al. 1986, Goodale et al. 1986, Paulignan et al. 1991, see also Brogaard 2011). In short, the subject's action trajectory changes as the perceptual representation of the target's location changes, but this change is not available to introspection. And this is true of all actions that require microadjustments to our ongoing action, which means it is true of most of our perceptually guided actions.

Most philosophers of action are interested in fairly complex actions – rational actions, moral actions, autonomous actions, and so on. And these are undoubtedly more interesting in some ways than the action of flossing or reaching for our cup on the table. But we can understand many aspects of the role actions play in our mental life better if we focus on these mundane actions, like flossing, and not on rational moral actions.

Take the example of voting out the current government. According to the standard account of motivation, which I'll go along with for the sake of simplicity, this action is motivated by various beliefs and desires of mine. I may believe that the current government does not do enough for social justice. And I may have a desire for a better government that represents me and my priorities better. These beliefs and desires lead to an intention and this intention leads to the perceptually guided action of ticking this specific box.

Many mental states go into the performance of this action. Beliefs, desires, intentions, and then the representation of action-properties without which there would be no action at all, and no change in the government. Some of these mental states are very much accessible to me. I would be happy to talk for hours about why the current government doesn't do enough about social justice, for example. But the representation that attributes action-properties is, as we have seen, not fully accessible. The representation of action-properties often changes without us noticing as it tracks the changes in the action-relevant features of the environment and we are often not aware of these changes. This means that some parts of our actions are not fully accessible to us.

I said that the vast majority of our bodily actions are perceptually guided. But why not all? Take the action of waking up in the middle of the night in your pitch-dark room and reaching to turn on the light. Is this a perceptually guided action?

On the face of it, this is not a perceptually guided action as I don't perceive anything. It's pitch dark and what allows me to reach to turn on the light is that I know where the light switch is, given that it's my bedroom. It seems that this is not a perceptually guided action.

But remember that an action is perceptually guided if it is guided by a perceptual representation. And as I will argue in Section 5.2, mental imagery is a form of perceptual representation, albeit one that is not directly triggered by sensory input. And in this example, what guides my action of switching on the light is my mental imagery that represents – very much perceptually – the layout of my room in the absence of any kind of sensory stimulation. So in this sense, this is a perceptually guided action. I will say more about the relation between perception and mental imagery in Chapter 5.

We know a fair amount about how this perceptual guidance of actions happens in the brain. The first thing to note is that talking about *the* visual system is misleading to begin with – our visual system (and the visual system of other mammals) is not a unified whole: it consists of two more or less separate visual subsystems: the dorsal and the ventral one. They both originate from the primary visual cortex but proceed in very different parts of the human brain. The main function of the dorsal stream is to help us perform various perceptually guided actions with the perceived objects. The main function of the ventral stream is to help us identify and recognize the perceived objects (see Goodale and Milner 2004, for an overview).

While these two subsystems normally work together, they can be, and in the case of some patients, they are, dissociated (although this is consistent with the rich bidirectional interactions between the two in normal cases, see Franz et al. 2000, Franz and Gegenfurtner 2008, Schenk and McIntosh 2010). Patients who have a more or less intact ventral stream, but a damaged dorsal stream, are very good at recognizing and identifying objects, but they find it difficult to perform perceptually guided actions with them or even to localize them in their egocentric space. And patients who have damage in the ventral stream but have a relatively intact dorsal stream can perform actions remarkably successfully with objects they can't identify or recognize (or even experience in some cases).

But the functioning of the ventral and the dorsal stream can be dissociated even in healthy human subjects – in the case of some optical illusions. One famous example is the 3D Ebbinghaus illusion. The 2D Ebbinghaus illusion is a simple optical illusion, familiar from various perception textbooks and popular science books: if a circle is surrounded by smaller circles, it looks bigger than a circle of the same size that is surrounded by larger circles (see Figure 4.1). The experienced size of the circle depends on the context we see it in – if it is surrounded by larger circles, we experience it as smaller. If it is surrounded by smaller circles, we experience it as bigger.

The 3D Ebbinghaus illusion is the very same illusion, in 3D, that is, with poker chips instead of circles. The experienced size of the poker chip depends on the context we see it in – if it is surrounded by larger poker chips, we experience it as smaller. If it is surrounded by smaller

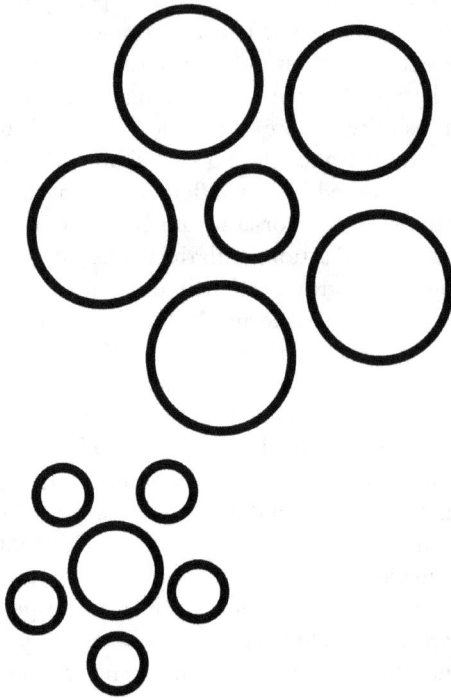

Figure 4.1 The 2D Ebbinghaus illusion.

circles, we experience it as bigger. But, and here is the surprising find-ing, if we are asked to reach out to pick up this poker chip, the grip size we approach it with is not (or only very mildly) influenced by the illu-sion. As it has been evocatively put, this optical illusion deceives the eye, but not the hand (Aglioti et al. 1995). The standard explanation for this effect is that while our ventral stream is deceived by this illusion and leads to the experience of the two poker chips as having different sizes, our dorsal stream is not deceived (or is much less deceived) – it leads to the dorsal representation of the size-properties of the poker chip as more or less the same (Aglioti et al. 1995, see also Goodale and Milner 2004, but see Schenk and McIntosh 2010 for some complications). In sum, sometimes the ventral stream and the dorsal stream attribute dif-ferent size properties to the very same object.

An interesting case where this happens is picture perception. Whenever we see a picture, we appear to see two different things at the same time: the picture surface and the depicted scene (Wollheim 2003, Nanay 2018d). When I look at a black and white photograph of an apple, the picture surface is flat, glossy and has various shades of gray. The depicted apple is not flat, not glossy and red. An important question both in psychology and in philosophy is how our perception works differently when we see an apple in a picture and not face to face (Lopes 1996). And one possible way of answering this question is exactly in terms of the dorsal/ventral distinction: our dorsal stream attributes properties to the picture surface and our ventral stream attributes properties to the depicted scene (Nanay 2008, 2011d, 2015c).

Leaving the picture perception case aside, it is important to emphasize that the distinction between the ventral and the dorsal streams of perceptual processing have their equivalent in other sense modalities as well (Kaas and Hackett 1999, Reed et al. 2005). Also, note that the function of the dorsal and the ventral streams correspond to the two functions of perception we have distinguished in Section 1.5: the dorsal stream helps us to perform actions and the ventral stream helps us to form beliefs that can later help us to perform actions.

4.4 PERCEPTION IS NOT ALL-PURPOSE

We have seen that perception often guides actions and that the action-relevant features of the environment are perceptually represented. This makes for a tight interaction between perception and action and one that by and large bypasses our higher cognitive abilities, like rational reasoning, belief formation or language.

This direct link from perception to action is, in many ways, a good thing. It allows us to react quickly and with great accuracy to the changes in our environment. But it's not all great news as this direct perception-action link is also the source of a number of our implicit biases – behavior that is inconsistent with our standing beliefs. For example, you may have very strong anti-racist beliefs, but because of this direct perception-action link, you nonetheless may stand a bit further away in the elevator from certain people with certain skin color (Dunham et al. 2008).

In this section, I will argue that perception and action are even more intertwined.

The first thing to note is that action does not only influence perception in the sense that perception represents the world in a way that is geared toward action performance. Depending on what action we want to perform, we perceive the world very differently. Suppose that you're looking at your phone. Your perception of the phone will be very different depending on whether you want to call a cab with it or drive in a nail with it.

Again, in some sense, this makes evolutionary sense. Not only does action shape our perception in a general sense, that is, in that perception represents action-properties. The kind of specific action we want to perform also determines the content of our specific perceptual state.

The most important and most directly relevant empirical finding that supports this claim is the following (Gutteling et al. 2015). The experimenters varied the action the subject intended to perform (grasping versus pointing at one of two small elongated black bars, one on the left and one on the right) and this action preparation influenced the early visual cortices (and even the primary visual cortex). It is important that the actions were not in fact executed: action preparation itself influenced early visual processing.

So what we want influences what we see. But one would want to know how this influence happens and what mediates between what we want and what we see. And my answer is that this mediator is attention.

What we want influences what we attend to and what we attend to influences what we see. The first half of this claim seems obvious: what we attend to depends on what action we intend to perform. I will attend to different features of my phone when I intend to call a cab with it and when I intend to drive in a nail with it. And we also know that the allocation of attention heavily influences not only the conscious perceptual experience (as shown by the inattentional blindness experiments we have encountered in Section 1.4), but attention modulates and influences processing already in the primary visual cortex (Gandhi et al. 1999, Murray et al. 2002, Kok et al. 2014) and even the thalamus (O'Connor et al. 2002). In short, what we want influences perceptual attention and perceptual attention influences early cortical perceptual processing. What we want influences what we see (Nanay 2006).

But there is yet another sense in which perception and action are deeply intertwined. In Section 4.2, I talked about how action influences perception. In Section 4.3, I talked about how perception influences and guides actions. I now want to talk about interaction between perception and action that goes both ways.

It would be tempting to think of perception as a completely passive process, where the traces of our environment are just imprinted on our sense organs, without us doing anything. But this is just false. Our perceptual system is in constant change to better capture the sensory input. And not only does it need to track the sensory input. It also needs to keep track of how it changes, in relation to the sensory input.

We have seen three examples of this in Sections 2.1, 2.3, and 2.4. The first one was eye movement. What allows us to see the entire visual scene in front of us is that our eyes dart around, bringing new parts of the visual scene into focus. And when we do this, our perceptual system needs to keep track of how our eyes move. You are looking at this book. But now your visual system notices a flash of light on the right. Your eyes move there and what used to be in your fovea (the book) is now at the left-hand side of your visual field. And what used to be at the right-hand side (the flash of light) is now in your fovea. This happens several times every second and your visual system needs to be able to keep track of what used to be where and how the visual field changed as a result of your eye movements.

Note the two-way influence between perception and action. Perception influences eye movements – it is because of the flash of light in the periphery that our eyes moved that way. And then, in turn, our eye movements influence our visual processing, making it possible to keep track of the objects in our visual field.

Similar considerations apply in the case of olfaction. We have seen that olfactory perception heavily relies on sniffing. The way we sniff influences the olfactory stimulus we receive: the interaction between the odorants in the air and the hairlike endings of the olfactory receptive cells is very different depending on whether our sniffing is quick and sharp or slow and deep.

And, just as in the case of eye movements and vision, the influence goes both ways: Unpleasant smells tend to trigger quick and sharp sniffing and pleasant smells tend to trigger slow and deep sniffing.

So sniffing influences the olfactory stimulus and the olfactory stimulus influences sniffing. The action (of sniffing) and the perception (of smell) are deeply intertwined.

Finally, in the case of touch, when you move your finger across the surface of a cheese grater, you can do this slowly or quickly (don't try this at home!). And your perceptual system calculates the layout of the cheese grater differently depending on the speed of your movement. The same changes in your tactile receptors indicate smaller or larger features depending on whether your hand movement is slower or faster. Here, again, the movement of our hand or fingers influences tactile perception. The influence in the other direction is less clear than it is in the case of vision or olfaction, partly because we rarely use tactile perception without other sense modalities. But even so, we do use larger and faster movements when we explore larger features by tactile perception only and we tend to use slower movements for smaller features, like the holes of the cheese grater (and that's a wise choice too).

Maybe the best illustration of this back and forth between perception and action comes from nonhuman animals, like cats and dogs, and the way they move their ears depending on what direction interesting auditory stimulus comes from. If there is a loud noise coming from behind, the ears automatically move in a way that would make them face backward, which then allows for the auditory system to pick up the auditory stimulus more efficiently. And depending on the orientation of the ear, this stimulus is processed differently.

In all these examples, action and perception are intertwined. When the perceptual system processes the sensory input, it constantly takes into consideration by means of what kind of perceptual action this sensory input was acquired. And this perceptual processing may, and often does, then adjust the perceptual action in a way that would allow for richer or more fine-grained perceptual input to be picked up.

4.5 EGOCENTRIC PERCEPTION

I have been using the term egocentric in a very specific sense in the last pages. Perception represents objects in one's egocentric space, as indexed to one's own bodily position and abilities, otherwise it could not guide one's actions. In this sense, perception, or at least action-guiding perception, is egocentric. What matters in action-guiding perception is how I myself can use the objects around me. In this sense, perception is all about me, me, me!

But not all perception is action-guiding and, consequently, not all perception is egocentric. We have seen how our perception changes depending on what action we want to perform: the perceptual representation of the phone will be very different depending on whether I want to call someone or I want to drive in a nail with it. But then what happens if I am just sitting on a park bench, looking around without wanting to perform any action whatsoever? If the action-oriented nature of perception depends on the action we want to perform, then if we don't want to perform any action, the perception will not be action-oriented. I will say a lot more about the special moments when this happens in Chapter 6.

It seems then that there are two ways of perceiving. The first is egocentric perception, when perception represents only those aspects of the space around you that are potentially useful for action performance. This way of perceiving is always indexed to you personally: to the spatial position you occupy, your current goals, your strength, your skills, and so on.

The second way of perceiving is not inflected by actions at all. It is not indexed to anyone: not relativized to anyone's spatial position, goals or other peculiarities. This is what happens, for example, when you are sitting on a bench in a park, without any particular need or desire to perform any action. These two ways of perceiving are clearly very different. But how are these two ways of perceiving related to one another? Is one of them somehow primary or more basic than the other?

It would be tempting to say that the action-free way of perceiving is the more primary and more basic and egocentric perception is somehow derived from it. After all, in egocentric perception, something extra is added to perception – your own spatial position, goals, and so on –, and the addition of these extra elements make the pure perception rather impure inasmuch as egocentric perception is relativized to all kinds of specific peculiarities.

I think we should resist the temptation to think of egocentric perception as derived. Egocentric perception is more basic both evolutionarily and in terms of individual development. Our distant ancestors must have been able to perceive egocentrically, otherwise they would not have been able to run away from predators or catch prey. It is much less obvious that they were even capable of action-free perception as action-free perception does not seem to serve any straightforward evolutionary purpose, but even if it does, its function must be much more indirect than that of egocentric perception, which has very clear evolutionary advantages.

Also, newborn babies very quickly learn to perceive the environment in an egocentric manner, which is necessary for the performance of even the most rudimentary actions, like reaching out their hands. The acquisition of the ability to perceive in an action-free manner comes much much later (Piaget 1928). In short, it is egocentric perception that is more basic and action-free perception must be derived from it in some way.

But this leaves us with a puzzle: why and how did we, both as a species in the course of evolution and as individuals in the course of child development, acquire the ability of action-free perception on top of egocentric perception? What are the perks of perceiving the world in an action-free manner?

In order to answer this question, I need to talk about the social aspects of perception. Perception clearly plays an important role in our social interactions. Remember the debate about what properties are perceived? One of the contested questions in these debates is whether emotional properties are perceptually represented (Döring 2007). When I look at your face, do I see sadness? Or do I see certain shape and color properties and only represent your sadness post-perceptually? If we go for the former option, then perception itself is, at least sometimes, thoroughly social.

The perception of emotions is a contested topic, but it is much less controversial that we can perceive some things as being relevant to someone else's action. In egocentric perception, I perceive things as being relevant to my own action. But sometimes I perceive things as being relevant to someone else's action. Perception of this kind is not self-centered, but rather other-centered (Southgate 2020, Nanay 2020a).

When you see a tiger right in front of you that is about to attack you, this is egocentric perception. When you see your neighbor watering his garden, and unbeknownst to him, a tiger sneaks up behind him, and is about to attack, how do you perceive the tiger?

You don't represent it egocentrically – you don't represent any feature of the tiger as relevant to your actions as you are safely behind your reinforced concrete fence. You don't represent it in an action-free manner either. Actions will be an integral part of your perceptual state of the tiger in this scenario, but these actions are not yours – they are your neighbor's actions. Your perceptual state is not indexed to your own spatial location or goals, but rather to your neighbor's spatial location and goals. This is a case of other-centric (not egocentric) perception.

It is easy to see how evolutionarily beneficial other-centric perception is: when you see the world from the point of view of someone else, this can help you in a variety of ways, regardless of whether this someone else is a friend or a foe. Other-centric perception can help you cooperate with your friends better. And it can also help you to take advantage of your foes.

In a celebrated experiment involving chimpanzees, the subordinate chimp was facing off with a dominant chimp (Hare et al. 2000). The way social interaction works in the chimpanzee world is that the dominant ones get the food. If the subordinate were to take food, the dominant would immediately take it away. The experimental setup was very clever: in some conditions, the food was out in the open, for both chimps to see. In these cases, the subordinate did nothing. But in some other conditions, where the food was placed in a way that it was visible to the subordinate but was occluded from the dominant, the subordinate did sneakily take the food. The bottom-line is that the subordinate chimp saw what the dominant saw (or, rather, what the dominant didn't see). This is a beautiful demonstration of the social advantages of other-centric perception.

Other-centered perception is somewhere halfway between egocentric perception and action-free perception. It is like egocentric perception inasmuch as it represents the world in an action-oriented manner. But it is unlike egocentric perception, inasmuch as it has nothing to do with one's own actions. And one way of explaining how action-free perception came about is to appeal to other-centric perception. Other-centric perception is, in some important sense, detached from one's own pragmatic interests (because it is all about someone else's pragmatic interests). But it is not completely detached from action. Nevertheless, given that in a complex social world we need to switch back and forth between different perspectives and different 'others' to center our perception around, this could pave the way to an even more detached form of perception, which is entirely action-free. More on this form of action-free perception in Chapter 6.

4.6 SUMMARY

Action is very important for survival – so we can expect natural selection to endow us with a perceptual system that is trying to maximize successful action performance. And the same goes for perception. In some sense, the perceptual system evolved to allow us to perform actions successfully. A major question about perception (and the function thereof) is how these action-oriented origins of perception shape the content of perceptual representations.

Conversely, we have plenty of empirical evidence that perception can directly, quickly, and often without the involvement of any conscious processes, lead to action. This causal link between perception and action is often so tight that it bypasses much of our cognitive apparatus. This has its problems when it comes to biased behavior (and ideological biases in general), but understanding this perception–action link also puts constraints on understanding how perception represents the world.

PERCEPTION WITHOUT INPUT

5.1 OFFLINE PERCEPTION

Close your eyes and visualize an apple. For most people – not everyone, see below – this mental action brings up some kind of visual experience that is somewhat similar to actually seeing an apple. Throughout the history of philosophy, the comparison between seeing and visualizing was an important theme, but there are other, arguably more important, similarities between seeing and visualizing than the similarity of the phenomenal feel.

Crucially, the activation of the visual cortices is also very similar (albeit not identical). When you see an apple, the contours of the outlines of an apple are represented in the primary visual cortex (Dijkstra et al. 2019). And when you visualize an apple, the same thing happens (I set aside some intriguing differences concerning which of the seven layers of the primary visual cortex are activated in the case of different vs. visualizing, see Kok et al. 2016).

Further, the eye movements and pupil dilation that accompany visualizing and seeing are also very similar (Laeng et al. 2014). When you see a triangle, your micro-saccades tend to follow the sides of the triangle. And the exact same thing happens when you visualize a triangle (see Section 5.4 for some details). As we have seen

DOI: 10.4324/9781032639536-5

in Section 2.1, eye movements are not mere by-products of vision: without eye movements, there would not be vision at all. And the same is true of visualizing: artificially blocking eye movements makes visualization close to impossible (Mast and Kosslyn 2002).

I have been focusing on visualizing, but the way the visual cortices are activated when we dream is also very similar to the way they do so in perception (Horikawa and Kamitani 2017). And our eye movements are also similar: our micro-saccades trace the outlines of the objects we dream about the same way they trace the outlines of perceived objects (see Section 5.4 for some details). And there is also phenomenal similarity between dreaming and perceiving.

The same is true of some forms of hallucination. Hallucination is a diverse phenomenon and different kinds of hallucinations have very different causes in the brain, but the most widespread forms of hallucinations involve early sensory activation. This normally happens in audition, but in the visual sense modality, for example, this early sensory activation corresponds to the outlines of the hallucinated scene (Kompus et al. 2013). The micro-saccades are also similar, as is the phenomenal feel that accompanies hallucinating and perceiving. In some extreme cases (although not in all cases of hallucination), it may even mislead us to think that we are in fact perceiving.

I will use the term 'offline perception' to cover all these cases: visualizing, dreaming, and hallucinating (Currie 1995, Fazekas et al. 2021). Offline perception is a technical term. It means running the perceptual apparatus in the absence of its normal input. The normal input of the visual perceptual apparatus is the retinal image. When you close your eyes and visualize an apple, there is no retinal image – no input. After all, your eyes are closed. But the perceptual processing that happens in this case is remarkably similar to the perceptual processing of the retinal image in the case of actually seeing an apple.

The same point applies to dreaming and hallucinations. There is no light hitting our retina when we're dreaming, but dreaming involves perceptual processing in the absence of any input. And although it is possible to hallucinate with our eyes wide open, in this case, this retinal image has little to do with the content of hallucination. If I am staring at the wall and hallucinate an apple, the hallucination is still not the perceptual processing of the sensory input (caused by the wall), but rather the processing that is remarkably similar to perceiving an apple (not a wall). This point also applies to visualizing with our eyes open.

In all these cases, the perceptual processing is very similar to bona fide perception. But in spite of these similarities, we very rarely confuse visualizing and dreaming with perceiving. Online and offline perception involve very similar perceptual processing. But there is a huge difference, namely, that in one case, this perceptual processing is the processing of the input, whereas in the other, it is not.

I said that offline perception is perception in the absence of its normal input. But what is normal here? Visual processing without retinal input is offline perception, as visual perception normally starts with retinal input. But, as we have seen, we can have offline perception even if there is retinal input, for example, when we are visualizing or hallucinating with our eyes open. Is this perception in the absence of its normal input? In some sense, it is not: there is normal input (the retinal image) and there is perceptual processing (visualizing or hallucinating with our eyes open).

But, and this is what is abnormal in these cases, the causal connection between the two is broken. The perceptual processing that amounts to visualizing or hallucinating with our eyes open is not directly triggered by the sensory input. In other words, what matters from the point of view of offline perception is not whether we have sensory input (as in some cases of offline perception we do), but rather whether the perceptual processing is directly triggered by the sensory input. If it is, it's online perception. If it's not, it's offline perception. The title of this chapter should be understood this way: this chapter is about perception without input that directly triggers the perceptual processing.

We replaced the rather vague phrase 'in the absence of normal input' with a better one about 'not directly triggered by input.' But is this really less vague? I hope so, but more needs to be said about what this amounts to. When you close your eyes and visualize an apple, the perceptual processing is triggered directly by some kind of top-down mechanism (involving the representation of an apple). It is not triggered, directly or indirectly, by the perceptual input (even if you visualize the apple while staring at your armchair).

But perceptual processing can also be triggered indirectly by perceptual input. When my eyes are closed but I am listening to the voice of someone I know, there is an involuntary activation of the visual perceptual processes, even the primary visual cortex (Vetter et al. 2014). And vice versa, when we watch the TV muted, there is involuntary activation of the auditory perceptual processes, even the primary auditory cortex. This is not direct triggering. In the muted TV case, the auditory processing is triggered, very much indirectly, by the visual input (of the TV screen). What would count as a direct trigger is the auditory input. But there is no auditory input – the TV is muted. The visual input is not a direct trigger: it triggers the perceptual processing indirectly (Pekkola et al. 2005).

More generally, perceptual processing is triggered directly by sensory input if it is triggered without the mediation of an extra representation. In the muted TV case, for example, the visual processing leads to a visual representation (in the early visual cortices) and this visual representation leads to the auditory representation. This mediating (visual) representation makes the triggering of auditory processing indirect. And this means it is offline perception. I will come back to the muted TV case in Section 5.5.

This chapter is about the importance of offline perception. And the reason why I included offline perception in this book is because in some sense it is a genuinely perceptual phenomenon. It is perceptual processing that leads to a perceptual representation. And this perceptual representation has the same format and very similar content as the kind of perceptual representation that we form on the basis of the processing of sensory input. No discussion of perception can ignore the various forms of offline perception.

5.2 MENTAL IMAGERY

I defined offline perception in Section 5.1 as perceptual processing that is not directly triggered by sensory input. This is extremely close to the way mental imagery is defined in psychology and neuroscience.

Here is a representative definition used in a recent review article on mental imagery in the leading journal *Trends in Cognitive Sciences*: "We use the term 'mental imagery' to refer to representations [...] of sensory information without a direct external stimulus" (Pearson et al. 2015, p. 590). This definition applies to visualizing but also to dreaming and hallucinating. The same goes for another influential definition, according to which "Visual mental imagery is 'seeing' in the absence of the appropriate immediate sensory input, auditory mental imagery is 'hearing' in the absence of the immediate sensory input, and so on" (Kosslyn et al., 1995, p. 1335). Again, this is true not just of visualizing, but also of hallucinating and dreaming.

I don't want to spend too much time on questions about labeling, but the way the term mental imagery is used in psychology and neuroscience seems interchangeable with offline perception. I will consider these concepts to be interchangeable in the rest of this chapter, but if someone has strong feelings about policing how the term mental imagery should or should not be used, they can just read offline perception whenever I say mental imagery (and think of dreaming and hallucinations as a subcategory of offline perception, but not of mental imagery). I will first talk about mental imagery in general and then turn to hallucinations and dreams.

The first thing to note is that while mental imagery is involved in closing your eyes and visualizing an apple, this way of exercising your mental imagery is atypical in a variety of ways (Nanay 2023).

The most trivial of these is that closing your eyes and visualizing an apple brings up visual imagery. But mental imagery can be auditory, olfactory, tactile, and so on. More generally, as perception is not necessarily visual perception, given that mental imagery is perceptual representation that is not triggered directly by the sensory input, mental imagery is not necessarily visual either.

Closing your eyes and visualizing an apple amounts to a voluntary act: you conjure up the mental imagery voluntarily. But we also often have involuntary mental imagery, for example, when we have a flashback to the scary scene in the film we watched yesterday. Earworms, auditory mental imagery of tunes we keep hearing in our head, are also involuntary. In short, mental imagery may be voluntary or involuntary.

Further, mental imagery may or may not be accompanied by a feeling of presence. When you close your eyes and visualize an apple, this imaginative episode is probably not accompanied by a feeling of presence. You are not deceived into thinking that there is actually an apple in front of you. But in some other instances of mental imagery, for example, in lucid dreaming or hallucination, this is exactly what happens. I will come back to this important phenomenon in Sections 5.3 and 5.4.

Mental imagery may also be more or less determinate (Nanay 2015a). When you close your eyes and visualize an apple, the mental imagery is likely to be fairly determinate: you have seen many apples in your life and if you really do put your mind into visualizing an apple, this is likely to bring up determinate mental imagery (but see the discussion of aphantasia below). But mental imagery can also be much less determinate, for example, when I try to recall the face of my first-grade math teacher, or, more generally, whenever I lack information about some features of what I have mental imagery of.

We have seen that mental imagery may be voluntary or involuntary. But it may also be conscious or unconscious. We have seen in Section 1.3 that perception may be conscious or unconscious. But as mental imagery is just a kind of perceptual representation – one that is not directly triggered by sensory input – mental imagery may also be conscious or unconscious (Phillips 2014, Koenig-Robert and Pearson 2020, Nanay 2021a). The possibility of unconscious mental imagery also makes it easier for us to account for a number of important features of what is known as aphantasia.

There is a recent body of research on subjects who report not having any conscious mental imagery whatsoever. This condition is called aphantasia (Zeman et al. 2010, 2015). A surprisingly large proportion of the population (according to some measures 5%–8%) have this condition: they lack conscious mental imagery: when they close their eyes and try to visualize an apple, no image is conjured up (while aphantasia is the most widespread in the visual sense modality, it also occurs in audition and the chemical senses).

Aphantasia is one end of the spectrum. On the other end of the spectrum we find people with extremely vivid imagery experiences – a condition often called hyperphantasia. Most of us are somewhere in between. And we know a fair amount about the neuroscience of what the vividness and precision of mental imagery depend on. There is a linear correlation between the vividness of mental imagery and some straightforward (and very easily measurable) physiological features of the subject's brain (such as the size of the subject's primary visual cortex and the relation between early cortical activities and the activities in the entire brain (see Cui et al. 2007; Bergmann et al. 2016).

Aphantasia is defined in terms of self-reports: if you say you don't have any conscious mental imagery, you are deemed to have aphantasia. But in terms of the actual causal mechanism, there is great diversity among aphantasia subjects. Many of them, for example, have no problem with involuntary mental imagery, but they can't conjure up mental imagery at will. Other aphantasia subjects have no conscious mental imagery whatsoever. However, there are some empirical reasons to believe that at least some of the aphantasia subjects, while they report no conscious mental imagery, do have unconscious mental imagery – unconscious perceptual representations that are not directly caused by the sensory input (Nanay 2021a).

But the ongoing research on aphantasia is important not only as a potential application of unconscious mental imagery. It highlights the enormous interpersonal variations in mental imagery. Some people – aphantasics – have no conscious mental imagery. Others – hyperphantasics – have extremely vivid mental imagery and these subjects often even mistakenly remember seeing or doing something that they merely imagined. These variations in the vividness of mental imagery (Kind 2017) should be a warning about taking our own conscious experiences of mental imagery as a starting point of theorizing about mental imagery.

A famous study on the vividness of the mental imagery of psychologists who work on mental imagery revealed that the theoretical position of these psychologists is predicted by the vividness of their mental imagery (Reisberg 2003). An advantage of taking mental imagery to be a technical notion (i.e., perceptual representation that is not triggered directly by sensory input) is to minimize these biases in our thinking about mental imagery.

I talked a lot about amodal completion in Section 2.1. Amodal completion in the visual sense modality is the perceptual representation of occluded parts of perceived objects. When you look at the image in the middle of Figure 2.3, your visual system completes this as the figure on the left and not as the figure on the right.

But what is this perceptual representation of the curved line behind the square? It is not sensory input-driven perception because we get no sensory stimulation from that curved line. It is perceptual representation that is not triggered directly by the sensory input. It is not triggered directly because what would trigger this representation directly would be the curved line across the square. But there is no sensory input of the curved line at all. And it is a perceptual representation because we know from many empirical studies that this representation of the curved line shows up already in the primary visual cortex (Lee and Nguyen 2001). In short, amodal completion amounts to perceptual representation that is not directly triggered by sensory input. Amodal completion is a form of mental imagery (Nanay 2010b).

Now, we have also seen that amodal completion is not a perceptual curiosity: it is a crucial feature of the vast majority of our perceptual states, because in almost all perceptual scenarios we see some objects behind and in front of other objects. And even on those occasions when we see, say, just one lonely spherical object in the middle of an empty room, our visual system still needs to complete the back side of this spherical object, from where we receive no visual input. It happens extremely rarely, only when looking at highly artificial two-dimensional visual displays, of, say, one red dot against a mono-chrome black background, that we do not use amodal completion. In all other cases, vision heavily relies on amodal completion.

Going further, while amodal completion is easier to demonstrate in the case of vision, it happens in all sense modalities (Nanay 2018b, 2022c). When you are talking to your friend on the street and a loud sports car passes by, some of what your friend says will be inaudible because in some moments, you only hear the engine noises of the sports car. Nonetheless, your auditory system fills in these gaps – mainly using top-down information. This feature of our auditory system is quite impressive. One demonstration of it is Jimmy Kimmel's segment 'A week in unnecessary censorship,' where completely innocent sentences uttered by famous politicians are beeped out in such a way that we can't help but auditorily complete them in a way that the beeped-out words sound like expletives. Amodal completion also plays a crucial role in tactile perception and olfaction (Young and Nanay 2022a).

In short, amodal completion is a nearly omnipresent feature of not just vision but also audition and all other sense modalities. If this is true, and if amodal completion really is a form of mental imagery, then mental imagery is a nearly omnipresent feature of perception. To put it simply, what we pretheoretically consider to be perception is in fact a hybrid of sensory input-driven perception and mental imagery. Perception is a hybrid of online and offline processing (see also Van Leeuwen 2011, Briscoe 2018, Brown 2018).

This is an important insight into the nature of perception and one that has various philosophical consequences. We have seen in Section 3.2 that many philosophers worry about the reliability of perception as a source of knowledge because of top-down influences on perception. We have also seen that these worries may not be fully justified. But if it is true that what we pretheoretically consider to be perception is in fact a hybrid of sensory input-driven perception and mental imagery, then we may have a more serious issue (Helton and Nanay 2019).

Sensory stimulus-driven perception is reliable inasmuch as there is a straight and unbroken causal chain from the light ray bouncing back from the object, hitting our retina and then directly triggering a perceptual representation. But in the case of mental imagery, by definition, this straight causal link is broken as mental imagery is perceptual representation that is not directly triggered by the sensory input. Because of this lack of direct trigger, there is always a degree of uncertainty about just how reliable the mental imagery component of perception is. To go back to the amodal completion example, the circular form may in fact continue behind the square as the figure on the right, but our visual system will nonetheless complete it as the figure on the left. And while amodal completion will get things right in the vast majority of cases, sometimes it won't.

Is this a reason to doubt the testimony of our senses? Not at all. But when talking about epistemology and the perceptual sources of knowledge, we should pay close attention to the empirical details of how those perceptual processes work that are not directly triggered by the sensory input. Epistemologists rarely pay attention to the nitty-gritty empirical details of how perception works. My point is that they should.

5.3 ILLUSIONS AND HALLUCINATION

Our thoughts and beliefs may or may not be correct. If I believe that Paris is the capital of Italy, then I have a false belief. Perception can also be correct or incorrect. When it is correct, we often say it is veridical. If perception represents something as having certain properties and this thing in fact does have these properties, then perception is veridical. But not all perceptual states are veridical – just as not all beliefs are true.

A standard distinction between two ways in which perception may be incorrect is between illusions and hallucinations. Suppose that you are looking at a red triangle and form a perceptual representation that attributes the shape property of being triangular and the color property of being red to the object in the middle of your visual field. In this case, your perception is veridical: your perceptual state represents a red triangle and there is in fact a red triangle in front of you.

But in less ideal cases, things can go wrong. Maybe the illumination is odd and you see the red triangle as orange. In this case, your perceptual representation attributes the shape property of being triangular and the color property of being orange to the object at the middle of your visual field. But the object there does not have the color property of being orange. It has the color property of being red. So your perceptual state misrepresents.

In the case of illusions, something goes wrong somewhere between the perceived object and your perceptual representation. But depending on where exactly in this causal chain things go wrong, we get different kinds of illusions. When the illusion is the product of odd illumination, this happens before the light hits your retina. In some sense, your visual system does exactly what it is supposed to be doing: given the orange sensory input, it comes up with a perceptual representation that attributes the color property of being orange to the triangle.

In some other cases, things go wrong in your retinal processing. One example is the Herman grid illusion (Figure 5.1), where the firing of retinal cells that correspond to the points where the white lines cross each other is influenced by the firing of nearby retinal cells in a way that trigger the illusion (of the dark circles there).

But the kinds of illusions I want to focus on are ones where things go astray between the sensory stimulation and the perceptual representation – as these would count as cases of mental imagery. These optical illusions depend on perceptual processes that are not directly triggered by sensory input. One example is the color spreading illusion: an optical illusion where we see a grid against a white background and some parts of the grid are colored dark gray, while the rest of the grid is lighter gray (see Figure 5.2). When seen from the right distance, those regions of the white background that are surrounded by the darker gray grid are perceived as (very light) gray.

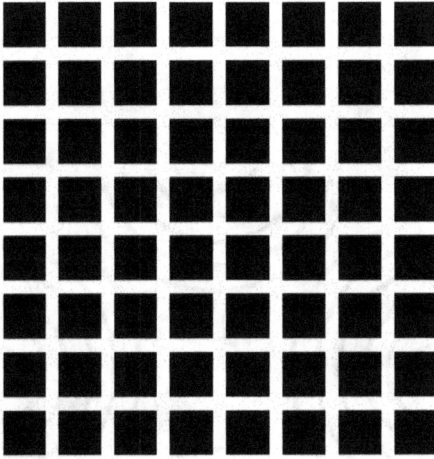

Figure 5.1 The Herman grid illusion.

Again, the perceptual representation of these illusory contours are not directly triggered by sensory input. We get monochrome white regions on the retina, but there is processing already in the early visual cortices and this leads to the experience of gray (Watanabe and Sato 1989) – thus the optical illusion.

We have seen that some – not all – instances of perceptual illusions count as mental imagery. In the case of illusions, the perceptual system attributes a property to an object that this object does not in fact have. We see a red triangle as orange, for example. But sometimes the perceptual system attributes a property to an object where it is not just that this object lacks the attributed property, but it doesn't exist at all. This is what we call hallucination. If my perceptual system attributes the color orange to a triangle in front of me and there is no triangle there at all, I hallucinate. To put it very simply, if the perceptual system misrepresents the attributed property, we get an illusion. If it misrepresents the object this attributed property is attributed to, we get hallucination.

Hallucination may seem pretty dramatic. While illusions are everywhere, one may think that hallucination only happens to people with mental health problems or in Shakespeare plays, where, for

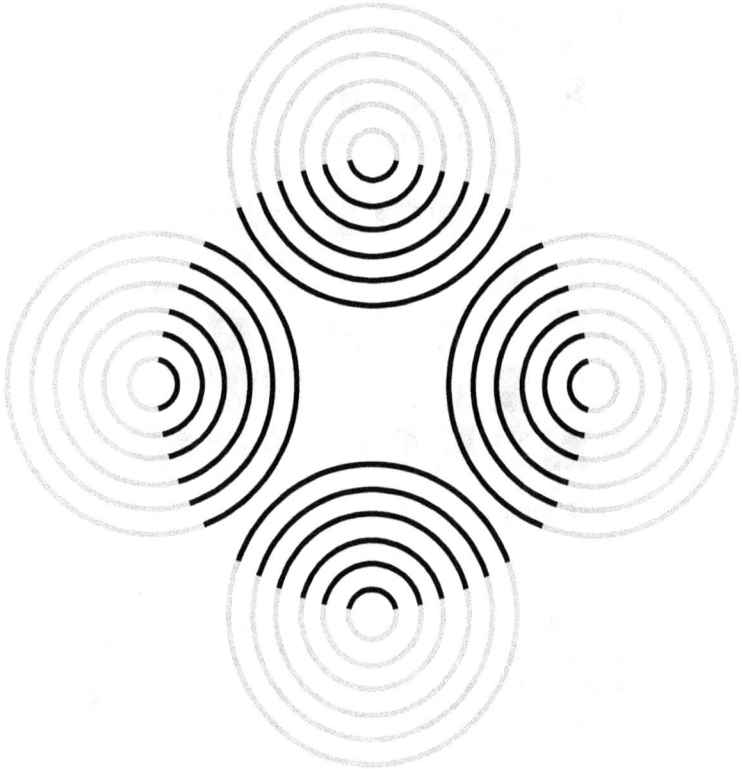

Figure 5.2 Color spreading illusion.

example, Macbeth hallucinates a bloody dagger when contemplating killing Duncan. In reality, most people hallucinate at least once a week (Linscott and van Os 2013). These hallucinations tend not to be as dramatic as Macbeth's and most of them happen in the auditory sense modality – two widely analyzed examples are hallucinating a voice when the toilet is flashed or when the fan is whirring. But hallucination is extremely widespread.

There are some conceptual issues in keeping apart veridical perception from illusions and illusions from hallucinations. First of all, in the example of the red triangle you see as orange, which I used in earlier paragraphs, while your perception is illusory with regards to color (orange instead of red), it is veridical in all other aspects: you see the object in front of you as a triangle and it is in fact a triangle, and so on. So this example is in fact a mixed illusory/veridical case. And we get a similarly blurry line between illusion and hallucination.

First of all, in psychiatry, the most widespread hallucinations are ones where it is not clear whether it is the attributed property that is misrepresented or the object it is attributed to is misrepresented. In fact, this applies to the two widely analyzed examples I used to introduce hallucinations two paragraphs ago. When we hear voices – often voices of people we know or knew – in noise patterns, for example, in the sound of the toilet flushing or the whirr of an electric fan, is this illusion or hallucination?

The answer will depend on the thorny issue (see Section 2.2) of what auditory properties are attributed to. If they are attributed to sounds (or maybe spatiotemporal regions), for example, then this will count as illusion: our auditory system attributes the wrong property, but what it attributes this wrong property to (the sound or the spatiotemporal region) nonetheless still exists. If auditory properties are attributed to ordinary objects, like electric fans or long deceased relatives, then this episode will count as hallucination: we seem to hear the long deceased relatives, but no such relative is around, only the electric fan.

We have seen that some perceptual illusions count as mental imagery. Crucially, many, maybe even most (albeit not all) instances of hallucinations would also count as mental imagery (see Allen 2015, Nanay 2016a for summaries). In the case of most hallucinations, things go astray between the sensory input and the perceptual representation, which means that hallucination of this kind amounts to perceptual representation that is not directly triggered by sensory input. And this way of thinking about hallucination also matches the use of this term in psychiatric practice. Here is the official medical definition of hallucination from the *American Psychological Association's Dictionary of Psychology*: "a false sensory perception that has the compelling sense of reality despite the absence of an external stimulus" (VandenBos 2007, p. 427) – very close to perceptual representation that is not directly triggered by sensory input.

Hallucinations form a very diverse set of mental phenomena. And some forms of hallucinations may not count as mental imagery – a potential example is verbal hallucination in schizophrenia, which seems to be brought about by activations of the parts of the brain that are responsible for inner speech (Frith and Done 1988, note, however, that there may be good reasons to consider inner speech to be a form of auditory mental imagery). Nonetheless, the early sensory cortices already misrepresent in the vast majority of hallucinations (see Kompus et al. 2011 for a meta-analysis and Allen et al. 2008 for a summary, see also Henkin et al. 2000 for some neuroimaging findings on hallucination in the less researched sense modalities of olfaction and taste), which make them genuine examples of mental imagery.

One unusual feature of hallucinations needs to be acknowledged – something that the official medical definition explicitly highlights: the strong feeling of presence that accompanies hallucinations. We have seen that mental imagery may or may not be accompanied by a feeling of presence. Visualizing an apple rarely is, but the mental imagery that is involved in amodal completion is – when it is conscious – usually accompanied by a feeling of presence. As are hallucinations. And also – the topic I am now turning to – dreams.

5.4 DREAMING

A piece of empirical finding that really made the headlines a couple of years ago was that we can (partially) reconstruct dreamed objects and scenes just from the activation of the early cortical regions (Horikawa and Kamitani 2017). So if I put you in an fMRI scanner and you fall asleep, I can tell not only whether you are dreaming, but also the outlines of your dream images.

This result made quite a splash because dreams are often thought to be the final frontier of fully private experiences – something you and only you know about. It turns out that this is not so. The experimenter may know your dreams better than you do (especially given that we tend to forget the majority of our dreams – see below).

In the context of this chapter, it is also important to note that dreams will count as mental imagery as they amount to perceptual representations (as we have seen, representations in the early sensory cortices) that are not directly triggered by sensory input. And some of the experimental findings about dreaming help us to understand some features of mental imagery in general.

If the study about (partially) reconstructing dream content was not enough myth-busting about dreams, here is another set of findings about two-way communicating while dreaming. This study focuses on one kind of dreaming, called lucid dreaming. During lucid dreaming, our eyes move rapidly, and we tend to have very vivid images in front of our eyes but often also a clear sense that we are in fact dreaming and sometimes even some form of control over what we dream. It was discovered that during lucid dreaming, subjects can remember and perform instructions given by the experimenters. So they can voluntarily move their eyes to communicate. And they are also aware of stimuli coming from the outside world. These two features of lucid dreaming make it possible for the experimenters to have genuine two-way communication with the dreaming subject. The experimenter asks a question, and the dreaming subject responds with the help of eye movements (Konkoly et al. 2021; see also Baird et al. 2021).

Lucid dreaming is an important phenomenon for at least two reasons. First, it is usually accompanied by an extremely vivid feeling of presence (Voss et al. 2013). We have seen that while some forms of mental imagery are accompanied by a feeling of presence (e.g., hallucinations), some others are not (e.g., visualizing an apple). In lucid dreaming, the feeling of presence that accompanies our mental imagery, according to self-reports, is much closer to what we get in perception.

This distinction was about self-reports, which, as we have seen repeatedly, we should always treat with suspicion. But a new body of findings about eye movements during dreaming gives a structurally similar result.

When we look at an object that moves slowly, our eyes track this movement with small and smooth micro-saccades. When we visualize an object moving, the eye movement is very different. There are no smooth small micro-saccades, but larger, often voluntarily triggered eye movements. In terms of eye movements, these are as different as it gets. Here is the question: how does our eye movement unfold while we are dreaming? And the answer is that it is very much like our smooth eye movements with small micro-saccades in perception and very different from the larger eye movements of visualizing (LaBerge et al. 2018).

It does not directly follow from these findings that the nature of eye movement somehow explains the feeling of presence that accompanies our mental imagery. Or the other way round: the feeling of presence explains the nature of eye movements. But the two do co-vary with each other. Perception: we get smooth micro-saccades and we get a feeling of presence. Dreaming: we also get both. Visualizing: we get neither.

We often remember our dreams. But not always. According to recent statistics, 45% of dreams are remembered, whereas in 22% of cases, there is no memory of any dream whatsoever. But how about the remaining 33%? In these cases, we remember that we had a dream, but remember absolutely nothing about the content of this dream (Siclari et al. 2013). Dreams of this kind are called contentless or white dreams. It is an open question in dream research whether the lack of any memory of these dreams is a shortcoming of our memory or maybe these dreams are, to begin with, lower quality in signal (like a grainy tv screen with muffled sound), so it is not possible to remember them (see Fazekas et al. 2019 for a summary).

What makes this question especially tricky is that episodic memory itself is a form of mental imagery. Episodic memory (remembering seeing, hearing or doing something, rather than merely remembering a fact) involves early perceptual processing (Brewin 2014), which is certainly not directly triggered by sensory input (see also Laeng et al. 2014 for a good summary of empirical evidence on the relation between mental imagery and episodic memory). So when we remember our dreams, we have mental imagery (the episodic memory) about mental imagery (our dream).

Dreaming has long been considered to be a form of mental imagery (starting at least the 17th century in Hobbes 1655, see also Walton 1990). But there is a related phenomenon that has become a major (and quite fashionable) research field recently: daydreaming or mind-wandering. Studies demonstrate that humans spend, on average, approximately half (!) of their day mind-wandering, which simply means one thought following another in a seemingly involuntary manner (Seli et al. 2018). That is a lot of time.

There are enormous interpersonal variations in how much time we spend mind-wandering and how much control we seem to have over where our train of thoughts takes us (or, rather, how often we try to interfere with this involuntary train of thought). And there are also some interpersonal variations concerning whether people report mental imagery during mind-wandering. But emerging neuroscientific evidence suggests that mind-wandering typically involves the involuntary triggering of mental imagery (Hung and Hsieh 2022).

So mental imagery is present when we look around. It is also present when we close our eyes and try to think of nothing. But it plays an important role in other mental processes as well. There are empirical reasons to think that when we want or crave something, what we want or crave is represented by means of mental imagery (Kavanagh et al. 2005). Mental imagery also plays a role in decision-making (Nanay 2016b). Very little of what goes on our mind happens without any involvement of mental imagery.

5.5 MULTIMODAL MENTAL IMAGERY

I want to close this chapter with a discussion of a special kind of mental imagery that plays a crucial role in perception: multimodal mental imagery. Remember that mental imagery is perceptual representation that is not directly triggered by the sensory input. One way in which this indirect triggering of the perceptual representation can happen is by means of a different sense modality.

This is what happens when you watch the TV muted: you get no auditory input, but, especially if you know the tone of voice of the person talking on TV, you will have auditory mental imagery. This is something you may even be consciously aware of, but even if you are not, there is early perceptual processing in your auditory system, which is not directly triggered by the auditory input – because the TV is muted. Instead, it is triggered by the visual input. In short, you have multimodal auditory mental imagery (Nanay 2018a).

Here is another example, described memorably by Marcel Proust (in *Le Coté de Guermantes*): when talking to someone you know very well on the phone, your visual system gets activated by this auditory input. This happens even if (and especially if) your eyes are closed: your visual perceptual processing is triggered indirectly by the auditory input. You have multimodal visual mental imagery.

Proust clearly had very vivid mental imagery, so he came to this conclusion on the basis of introspection. But recent empirical findings give the same result (Vetter et al. 2014). In these studies, subjects were blindfolded and they listened to distinctive sounds – birds chirping, people chattering, cars driving by. And their primary visual cortex was scanned while they were listening to these sounds. The crucial result is that these sounds could be distinguished on the basis of the activities of the primary visual cortex alone. So each time we hear some kind of sound we are familiar with, multimodal visual imagery (in the sense of visual processing triggered by auditory input) gets triggered.

Remember that in Section 5.2, I argued that as amodal completion is present in almost all of our perceptual episodes, and as amodal completion is a form of mental imagery, mental imagery is present in almost all of our perceptual episodes. We can now see that multimodal mental imagery gives us an additional reason why mental imagery plays a crucial role in perception in general.

Most of what we perceive we perceive via more than one sense modality. We both see and hear people, coffee machines and cats, and we can smell and touch them too. But it happens relatively rarely that we get information about something via all the possible sense modalities. More often, at least one of the sense modalities that could carry some information about the object is silent. In this case, the other sense modalities induce early processing in this input-less sense modality and this amounts to multimodal mental imagery. This is, besides amodal completion, another major source of the importance of mental imagery in everyday perception.

Multimodal mental imagery can also help us to explain a number of perceptual phenomena that I have discussed in earlier chapters of this book. Sensory substitution is a prime example. We have seen in Section 2.2 that blind people can navigate their environment surprisingly well with the help of sensory substitution devices (a camera on one's head that transfers its images real time to little pricks on one's skin). I spent some time in Section 2.2 examining whether this amounts to vision or tactile perception. If sense modalities are individuated according to the sense organs involved, it seems that it is touch. If they are individuated according to phenomenology, then some subjective reports of people using sensory substitution devices suggest it may be vision.

In the light of the concept of multimodal mental imagery, we can now see that sensory substituted 'vision' is neither vision nor tactile perception. It is not perception at all. It is multimodal mental imagery. It is perceptual representation in the visual sense modality (and we now know that this can happen as early as the primary visual cortex, see Murphy et al. 2016) that is triggered by the sensory input in another sense modality, namely, tactile perception. Which means that it is an instance of multimodal mental imagery: visual representation triggered by tactile input (Nanay 2017).

To stick with the visually impaired, braille reading is also a form of multimodal mental imagery: when blind people read braille, their visual cortex is extremely active (Burton 2003). So this is another example of visual perceptual representation that is triggered by tactile input. In other words, it is another instance of multimodal mental imagery.

As we have seen in Section 2.5, echolocation is another technique that blind people can learn in order to navigate their environment. And recent findings show that echolocation also uses early visual resources (Norman and Thaler 2019). So the blind subject makes clicking noises and the auditory input of the reverberation triggers visual perceptual representations. Again, perceptual representation in one sense modality (vision) is triggered by input in another sense modality (audition).

I have been talking about visual perceptual representations of blind people and this may raise eyebrows. But it should not. Many blind people often have quite vivid visual mental imagery (Villey 1930). More generally, blindness is not a monolithic phenomenon: to simplify a bit, it can be caused by some kind of irregularities in the eye or by some kind of irregularities in the visual cortices. The latter is called 'cortical blindness' and it is relatively rare. But if the problem is with the eye, then the visual cortex can function as well as it used to (especially if the subject became blind relatively late in life). So while perceptual representations in visual processing can't be triggered by visual input – there is no visual input, given that the subject is blind – they can be triggered by input in different sense modalities. And many techniques that can really help blind people get around are based on exactly such multimodal mental imagery.

A widespread phenomenon where multimodal mental imagery really helps us to understand what is going on is synesthesia. Some synesthetes hear a musical note and experience it as having a specific color (Ward et al. 2006). Some others experience a specific color each time they see a specific black numeral or letter printed on white background (Jonas et al. 2011). Synesthesia comes in various different forms, often linking different sense modalities with one another (Sagiv et al. 2006, Tang et al. 2008).

And this linking of different sense modalities is of a very specific kind. When we look at the ways synesthesia is defined in the empirical literature, it is difficult not to notice a pattern, especially in the light of the concept of multimodal mental imagery. Here are some representative examples: "stimulation of one sensory domain leading to a perception in another sensory domain" (Harrison and Baron-Cohen 1997), "the elicitation of perceptual experiences in the absence of the normal sensory stimulation" (Ward and Mattingley 2006), and "stimulation in one sensory or cognitive streams [that] leads to associated experiences in a second unstimulated stream" (Simner 2012). These definitions are strikingly similar to the definition of mental imagery (the Ward and Mattingley 2006 definition) or multimodal mental imagery (the other two definitions).

Importantly, synesthesia involves activation of the early cortical areas of the synesthetically activated sense modalities or 'sensory streams.' If synesthetes have a color experience when hearing a certain pitch, there will be perceptual processing in their visual sense modality (Barnett et al. 2008), and we also know that in most cases, this is early perceptual processing in the primary sensory cortices (see, e.g., Nunn et al. 2002, Hubbard et al. 2005, Jones et al. 2011). As this early perceptual processing is not directly triggered by sensory input, this is an instance of mental imagery (Nanay 2021b).

Mental imagery in general and multimodal mental imagery in particular play a crucial role not just in our everyday perception (because of amodal and multimodal completion) but also in understanding a variety of perceptual curiosities. We can't understand what perception is without understanding how online and offline perception are combined to give us a fuller, more complete representation of the world.

5.6 SUMMARY

In standard cases, perception starts with sensory input. But perceptual processing often happens without being triggered by the sensory input. This phenomenon is sometimes referred to as offline perception. This is what happens when we dream or hallucinate and in the various uses of mental imagery.

Perception without input – offline perception – is often combined with input-driven perception in our everyday perceptual experiences. This gives rise to a hybrid offline/online perception, which has been an influential thought in the history of philosophy, but which is also supported by a variety of empirical findings from neuroscience and psychology.

6

AESTHETIC PERCEPTION

6.1 AESTHETIC EXPERIENCE

I talked a lot about the function of perception: about what perception is used for. But perception is not always geared toward survival. In fact, in those moments in life we care about the most, it is often entirely function-less. This last chapter is about those perceptual episodes that we treasure but that are not about enhancing our chances of reproductive success by means of guiding actions or justifying beliefs. This last chapter is about aesthetic perception.

Aesthetic experiences are special kinds of experiences. Note that while I have deliberately avoided talking about experiences in the first five chapters of the book and made a deliberate effort to be neutral about whether perception is conscious or unconscious, I now focus on conscious perceptual experiences. The reason for this is that this chapter is about perceptual experiences that we are very much conscious of: aesthetic experiences.

As a starting point, it is important to make a distinction between aesthetic experiences and the experiences of artworks. When aesthetics as a discipline was born in the 18th century, it was taken to be the science of sense perceptions (Baumgarten 1758). In short, aesthetics is about special kinds of experiences. It is very different

DOI: 10.4324/9781032639536-6

from philosophy of art, which is about art. We should not confuse the two. We can have very prosaic experiences of artworks, for example, when an art dealer is trying to assess how much profit they can make if they bought a certain artwork, or, when an art thief is trying to smuggle the artwork out of the museum. In short, not all experiences of artworks are aesthetic experiences.

Conversely, not all aesthetic experiences are experiences of artworks. We often have aesthetic experiences of nature, but also of everyday scenes, like the random arrangements of bottles on a kitchen table, the autumn leaves in the park on our way home from work or even just the light of the setting sun falling on the bedroom wall. Questions about what art is and what it is not, or what the meaning of an artwork depends on, may be important in the philosophy of art, but they have little to do with perception. Questions about aesthetic experiences, in contrast, have an awful lot to do with perception.

Aesthetic experiences are special kinds of experiences we really care about. And many of our aesthetic experiences will be strong, powerful, awe-inspiring experiences. But not all. The experience that makes you choose the shirt you're going to wear today or that makes you wonder whether you should put more pepper in the soup could also be an aesthetic experience. Aesthetic experiences are everywhere. They are extremely important aspects of our life.

Given that this is a book on perception, I will spend a lot of time talking about aesthetic experiences that are perceptual experiences. But I do not mean to suggest that all aesthetic experiences are automatically perceptual. While I do think that many of them are – and some of the personally most valuable ones also tend to be – I want to leave open the possibility that maybe one can have an aesthetic experience of a beautiful mathematical theory or an unexpected turn in a philosophical argument. I want to bracket these cases from now on and focus on perceptual aesthetic experiences (I'll return to these questions in Section 6.3).

We have seen the extent of cross-cultural and individual differences in perception, resulting from top-down influences on perception. So we should expect cross-cultural and individual differences in aesthetic experiences as well (see Section 6.4 for more such differences in the aesthetic context). Hence, it would be futile to look for the characterization of the one true kind of aesthetic experience because there are many kinds of aesthetic experiences.

One of the perks of understanding the nuances of how perception works is that we are in a better position to characterize aesthetic experiences. I will focus on a form of aesthetic experience that has been extremely influential and common since roughly the 18th century. I want to explicitly acknowledge that aesthetic experiences may have been very different in earlier time periods and even in this time period, there are significant variations between different parts of the world (Nanay 2019, 2022d, forthcoming b).

Here are two representative quotes from two writers who were very good at describing complex perceptual experiences. The first one is from Marcel Proust:

> But even the ugliness of faces, which of course were mostly familiar to him, seemed something new and uncanny, now that their features, – instead of being to him symbols of practical utility in the identification of this or that man, who until then had represented merely so many pleasures to be sought after, boredoms to be avoided, or courtesies to be acknowledged – were at rest, measurable by aesthetic coordinates alone, in the autonomy of their curves and angles.
>
> (*Swann's Way* (trans. C. K. Scott Moncrieff). New York: Modern Library, 1928, pp. 469–470)

And the second one is from Albert Camus:

> In the cloisters of San Francisco in Fiesole, a little courtyard with arcades. Red flowers, sunshine and yellow and black bees. In a corner, a green watering can. Flies humming everywhere. In the warmth, the little garden breathes gently. [...] I want nothing else but this detachment and this closed space – this lucid and patient intensity.
>
> (*Carnets*, 1937, September 15)

Experiences of this kind are among the most important ones we have. But what is going on in our mind when we have them? One important perk of having a firm grasp on the various aspects of perception is that we can use this conceptual apparatus to explain some touchy-feely phenomena, like aesthetic experiences. The main player in this context will be the concept of attention.

6.2 AESTHETIC ATTENTION

We have seen in Section 1.4 just how much difference the allocation of attention can make in our experience in general. And this is also true of our aesthetic experience. So an important and influential way of specifying what is special about aesthetic experiences is that our attention is used differently.

In the inattentional blindness experiments we have encountered in Section 1.4, whether you are attending to the counting task makes a huge difference – it makes you miss the guy in the gorilla costume, which, if you're not attending to the counting task, is a central, salient part of your experience. So moving your attention around changes your experience.

But moving your attention around can also make an aesthetic difference in your experience. Look at Figure 6.1. It's a 15th-century painting representing Mary with Jesus and St John. It was painted by Domenico Ghirlandaio.

Now look at it again. Do you see the odd flying object in the sky? If you now look at the picture, it is difficult not to attend to it and wonder what it might be (something art historians are not entirely sure about).

In this case, attention is probably making a negative difference. Your attention is captured by this unidentified flying object and this is likely to interfere with the engagement of the central theme of the painting. But attention can also make a positive difference.

Look at the following piece by Paul Klee from 1927 (see Figure 6.2). It's a face, quite asymmetrical, weird eyes, an even weirder mouth. Now I can tell you the title: The mask with the flag. The vast majority of people who look at this image do not notice the flag in the upper left corner. Maybe you did, in which case, well done. But if you didn't, attending to it can completely transform your experience of the picture. Maybe it was unbalanced before, but now that you attend to the flag, it becomes balanced (this seems to be the kind of effect Klee went in for, see his *Pedagogisches Skitzenbuch* (Munchen: Langen), 1925). So here, attending to the flag is likely to make a positive difference.

Figure 6.1 Domenico Ghirlandaio: Madonna with Jesus and Giovannino.

There are many features an artwork has that are such that if you attend to them, this makes an aesthetic difference. Not necessarily a positive aesthetic difference, as we have seen, but an aesthetic difference nonetheless. I will call such features "aesthetically relevant features" (Nanay 2016c). Aesthetically relevant features can be very simple, like the flag in the Klee picture. But they can also be more complex, like the threefold symmetry in Domenico Veneziano's *Annunciation* (Figure 6.3), where one aesthetically relevant feature

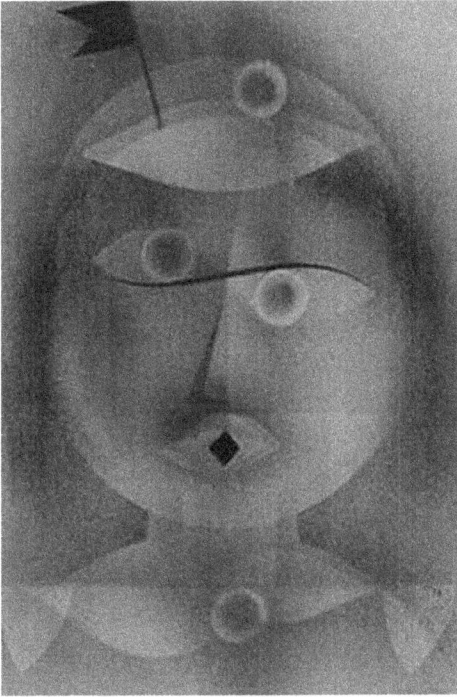

Figure 6.2 Paul Klee: The mask with the flag, 1927.

Figure 6.3 Domenico Veneziano: *Annunciation.*

is that the axis of symmetry of the picture itself is slightly different from the axis of symmetry of the building and both of these are different from the axis of symmetry of the depicted action. Attending to the relation between these three axes of symmetry can make a real aesthetic difference.

In all these examples, the attention that plays a role is perceptual attention, and the aesthetically relevant feature is perceived. And in many cases, aesthetically relevant features are indeed perceptually represented. But not always. They can be represented by higher-level, non-perceptual (cognitive) states, for example, when we know something about the artist's religious beliefs or mental illness, and this makes an aesthetic difference. In this case, the aesthetically relevant feature is not perceived. I will say more about a third category of aesthetically relevant features, ones that are represented in mental imagery, in Section 6.4.

So far, I have been focusing on the importance of what we are attending to. What we are attending to can make a real aesthetic difference. But it may be even more important how we attend. As Marcel Proust said, 'Attention can take various forms and the job of the artist is to evoke the most superior of these' (Marcel Proust: *Sodom and Gomorrah*, chapter II, paragraph 25 (p. 138 in the Moncrieff translation)).

And historically the main candidate for this 'superior' form of attending, as Proust would put it, is disinterested attention (Kant 1790/1928, Stolnitz 1960, but see also Dickie 1964s criticism). The general picture is that while our attention is 'interested' most of the time − it is in the service of the various tasks we are performing − when we have an aesthetic experience, attention is detached from these tasks and it is disinterested. This sounds great as a metaphor, but what does it mean that one's attention is disinterested? Understanding the nuances of our perceptual apparatus can help here as well.

I want to start with a distinction that is widely used in vision science between focused and distributed attention (Mack 2002). In simple attentional tasks, this distinction is straightforward enough: our attention is focused when we are following one small dot with our eyes as it moves across the screen. Our attention is distributed when we are trying to keep track of five different dots at the same time as they move around. These are different ways of attending.

This distinction is between focused and distributed attention to objects. But we can make a parallel distinction between focused and distributed attention to features. We can focus our attention on just one feature of the objects around us: say, we only attend to whether they are stripy. This is what happens when we try to spot Waldo in the *Where's Waldo* books. And we can also distribute our attention across different features of an object.

This gives us four ways of attending (Nanay 2015b):

(a) Attention to one feature of one object (object: focused, features: focused). This is the kind of attention we use in demanding attentional tasks, like tying a difficult knot.
(b) Attention to one feature of many objects (object: distributed, features: focused). This form of attention is used in visual search (like the Where's Waldo puzzles).
(c) Attention to many features of many objects (object: distributed: features: distributed). Given the limitation of the attentional bandwidth of the human mind, this is not really an actual option as we can't seem to attend to more than five things at the same time (Alvarez and Franconeri 2007).
(d) Attention is focused on one object but distributed across many of its features (object: focused, features: distributed).

It is this last category, where we focus our attention on one object, but our attention is distributed across many of its features, which characterizes many (albeit not all) of our aesthetic experiences. One may think that disinterested attention is a contradiction in terms: attention indicates some kind of focus, but disinterestedness indicates a lack of focus. In the light of the fourfold distinction I just made, we can make sense of this seemingly contradictory form of attention: it is disinterested in the sense that the attention is distributed across the features of the object, but it is attention in the sense that it is focused on one and only one object.

This way of attending is a crucial ingredient of a plausible description of many (again, not all) of our aesthetic experiences. But it is a description, not a recipe. It does not guarantee that you have an aesthetic experience. And, in fact, nothing does — maybe that's why we spend so much time and money pursuing aesthetic experiences (Lopes et al. 2021, Nanay forthcoming d).

Aesthetic experiences are fickle things. It happens a lot that you are listening to a song that you normally have aesthetic experience of, but this time nothing is happening. Maybe you're too preoccupied with something else. Or maybe you're just too sleepy. But the aesthetic experience is just not coming. This itself is a crucial feature of aesthetic experiences, namely, that they are not fully under our control. And the central role of attention in aesthetic experiences can at least partially explain this as attention is not fully under our control.

I argued that attention that is focused on one object but distributed across many of its features is a crucial ingredient of aesthetic experiences. But it does not fully explain these kinds of experiences. There is an extra aspect of our attention in aesthetic context: it is free and open-ended.

Imagine that your car has broken down. You open the hood to look for the problem. In some sense, your attention is focused on one object (on the car's engine and its various parts) and distributed across its various features. But this is very far from being an aesthetic experience. What is missing is the open-endedness of your experience. While your attention is distributed across many features, it is not at all free or open-ended as you're only attending to what could possibly help you fix the problem. So in that sense, attention that is not open-ended is not genuinely distributed.

I am not saying that this form of distributed attention is a universal feature of all aesthetic experiences. You may have had aesthetic experiences that are all about being fully absorbed and sucked up in an experience. And I have no intention to deny that this could be a genuine aesthetic experience. But many of our aesthetic experiences are open-ended in the sense I was trying to outline. And this form of open-ended aesthetic experience is what writers like Proust were trying to capture.

In aesthetic experiences of this kind, attention roams free. It is not trying to complete any quest. It is unconstrained. Any feature of the painting you are looking at could be relevant and your attention could bounce around among these properties unconstrained. In this sense, aesthetic experiences liberate our perception – a topic I will come back to in Section 6.5.

6.3 CROSS-CULTURAL AESTHETIC DIFFERENCES

In much of our aesthetic endeavors, we engage with objects that were created long ago or far away. We watch silent films, listen to Baroque music, read 12th-century Japanese novels, go to exhibitions of prehistoric or Mayan art. We often have aesthetic experiences when we do so.

But this raises an important question. When I, someone who has spent the vast majority of his time in Europe and North America, have an experience of, say, a ceremonial sculpture from Micronesia, will this experience be different from the aesthetic experience of someone who grew up in Micronesia?

The answer in the light of everything we know about perception is that it must be a different experience, and often a radically different one. And the reason for this is our old friend from Section 3.2, the top-down influences on perception. As we have seen there, perceptual processing is not a one-way street. It unfolds very differently depending on one's higher-level mental states. But given that people who grew up in different environments and different cultural milieus have different higher-level mental states, their perceptual processes will also be very different. Given the top-down influences on perception, cross-cultural variation is the norm, not the exception.

And the same goes for cross-cultural aesthetic variations. Take perceptual learning. As we have seen in Section 3.2, our perceptual state now heavily depends on our perceptual history. Remember Figure 2.2a? Depending on whether Figure 2.2b was part of our perceptual history, Figure 2.2a is experienced very differently. And people who grew up in very different places with different environmental features will have very different perceptual histories. Hence, their current perceptual state will also be significantly different.

Importantly, from the point of view of aesthetics, our perceptual history of aesthetic stuff heavily influences our current aesthetic experience. If you have spent decades listening to atonal free jazz, your experience of a free jazz piece will be very different from someone's who has only listened to 80s pop. And someone who has grown up appreciating Japanese tea ceremonies will have a very different aesthetic experience of them from someone who does this as a tourist for the first time. Our perceptual history influences our perception, and our aesthetic history influences our aesthetic experiences. As a result, we can never assume that if we have an aesthetic experience of an object, say, the ceremonial sculpture from Micronesia, someone with a very different cultural background will have the same kind of aesthetic experience. Their aesthetic experience may be radically different from ours.

But the importance of perceptual history is relevant in understanding our aesthetic engagement with artifacts from different cultural milieus for yet another reason. It is tempting to think that while there are cultural differences in aesthetic engagement, we can bridge this gap if we really put our minds to it. We can read up on the art of the Mayas, maybe move to the Yucatan to immerse ourselves in the environment where the Mayas lived. And this is, in fact, what many art historians who study the work of non-Western art, do. They deliberately change their perceptual history in a way that would be more similar to that of the original producers and consumers of the artifacts they study (Elkin 2006).

This is a commendable move, but it should be clear that it will never lead to the same kind of experience as the original producers and consumers of the artifacts had. And the reason for this, again, has a lot to do with the importance of perceptual history. Even if you are exposed to the kind of stimulus that is crucial for the relevant, say, contemporary Indonesian perceptual history, you will never be able to delete your own, presumably Western, perceptual history. So you will always see this artifact at least partly through your very much Western lenses – something that the original producers and consumers of the artifacts obviously did not have. This is not a reason to just throw up one's hands and give up. Studying and being exposed to cultures that are different from our own can be immensely valuable. But we should not have the illusion that we'll ever be able to replicate the aesthetic experiences of those who grew up in that culture.

Here is an example. This is a Haida carving from Northern British Columbia (Figure 6.4). Haida carvings are extremely complex. A wide range of animals, from the beaver to the dolphin, are depicted in a manner that, at first glance, may look very similar. And there are various not-so-easy-to-spot markers that indicate which animal is depicted. Beavers, for example, often (not always) have two elongated rectangles indicating their teeth. Hawks tend to have pointed ears. And so on.

Figure 6.4 Haida wood carving.

The anthropologist Franz Boas spent a very long time among the Haidas and on the basis of conversations with the local carvers, he had an extremely sophisticated understanding of the Haida system of depiction. But he observed that when he showed the very same design to carvers who lived in neighboring villages, or even two carvers in the same village but from different generations, they often gave very different descriptions of the depicted animals (Boas 1927). One said sea monster, the other one bear. This shows that extremely small nuances can make a huge difference not just in how one sees these carvings, but also in whether one sees a sea monster or a bear in them. And those who have little or no familiarity with Haida art will see these carvings very differently from either of these (Nanay forthcoming c).

This difference is, arguably, a result of a difference in attention. Let's go back to Figure 6.4. This is one of the sides of a rectangular box and this genre has fairly strict compositional rules. The image is of a grizzly bear, but if you don't know where to attend, it would be easy to mistake it for an image of a sea monster. In Haida iconography, sea monsters are depicted as something of a mix between a bear and a killer whale: it is a hybrid of some bear features and some killer whale features. And the salience of these components can vary. In the vast majority of carvings that are found on the sides of rectangular boxes, the head takes up almost the entire surface, as is the case here. As a result, very minor markers typical of the depiction of a killer whale, most typically, the dorsal fins, which could be tucked away in a corner, could make a major aesthetic difference. Depending on where you look, you would see a very different creature in the picture. To make things worse, the Tlingits, who live North of the Haidas in the Pacific Northwest, have very similar, but slightly different, conventions in their carvings on rectangular boxes, so they would attend to slightly different features of Figure 6.4. And someone who grew up in Europe, without much exposure to the art of the Pacific Northwest would, presumably, see some odd vaguely art deco pattern in the picture.

Can we reverse or cancel out the effects of perceptual learning? It seems that we can, at least locally (Becker and Rinck 2016). But these reversal techniques only work for cancelling out very specific stimuli. In order to revert the effects of decades of perceptual learning on our global aesthetic preferences in general, we would need decades of reversal training. More worryingly, perceptual learning is not linear. Exposure in childhood has a much more significant effect on our later processing and preferences than later exposure (although often not on childhood preferences, see Bowker and Sawyers 1988, Bornstein 1989, Rubenstein et al. 1999). This early perceptual learning process cannot be reversed or fully counteracted later in life.

It is important to emphasize that the more specific a certain experience is, the better chances we have to get close to the experience a participant would have. We have some experimental results about how perceptual learning is easier to reverse if we restrict the domain of the experience that we are trying to learn or unlearn (Becker and Rinck 2016). So we can make great progress acquiring the perceptual history of looking at a very specific kind of objects, say, the depiction of sea monsters in Haida carvings, which would be quite similar to the perceptual history of a Haida participant. But that is a very narrow slice of my (and the Haida participant's) entire perceptual history and the rest of our perceptual history will still diverge.

To sum up, aesthetic experiences of people with different cultural backgrounds differ because their attention differs. I will examine another important source of cross-cultural differences in Section 6.4: Aesthetic imagery.

But already now it is worth noting the fairly radical consequences of these cross-cultural aesthetic differences. It is tempting to think, or at least assume, that if I have an aesthetic experience of an object, everyone else, regardless of where and when they live or lived, would or maybe should have the same aesthetic experience. In fact, Immanuel Kant's famous dictum about the universal validity of aesthetic judgments (Kant 1790/1928, p. 52) comes close to saying a version of this. But in the light of the empirical findings about the top-down influences on perception and of the importance of perceptual history and of attention in aesthetics, this is just not true. People who grew up in different parts of the world will have very different aesthetic experiences of the very same object. So demanding or assuming that everyone would have the same aesthetic experiences as I do is an extremely arrogant attitude. Instead, we should approach all objects that were created in different cultural milieus with aesthetic humility (Nanay 2019, Lopes et al. 2024).

6.4 AESTHETIC IMAGERY

Attending to certain features of an artwork makes an aesthetic difference. In Section 6.2, I left open the question about just how these features are represented. Some of them, in fact, very many of them, including the examples in Figures 6.1, 6.2, and 6.3, are perceptually represented. We do see the odd black patch in the sky in Figure 6.1. We also see the flag in the upper left corner of the Klee painting (Figure 6.2). And while the interaction of the three axes of symmetry in Figure 6.3 is quite complex, it is nonetheless perceptually represented.

We have seen that some features of the artwork, like what social milieu it was created in or the mental health of the person who created it, could also be aesthetically relevant features, but they are not perceptually represented. Attending to them can make an aesthetic difference – you could see some aspects of the artwork differently if you knew that the artist was schizophrenic, for example, but the feature of being painted by someone with schizophrenia is not a perceptually represented feature.

But aesthetically relevant features are also often represented in mental imagery (Nanay forthcoming e). One very simple example of this in the visual arts is the mental imagery we use to extrapolate the depicted space beyond the frame of paintings or drawings (Burch 1973).

Let me make this point with the help of an example. Buster Keaton's 1923 short film *Cops* starts with this image (Figure 6.5). So when you go to the cinema and the film starts rolling, you know the title of the film, *Cops*, and you see this image. What kind of mental imagery will you form of what is beyond the frame of the image? Given the expectations created by the title of the film and the image of Buster Keaton behind bars, you are pushed to form mental imagery of a jail.

The film very clearly assumes that you have exactly this kind of mental imagery. In the second shot, it is revealed that Buster is not in jail, but he is standing behind a garden gate. And his face has that dejected expression not because he is locked up, but because he was

Figure 6.5 The first image of Buster Keaton: *Cops* (1923).

just rejected by the girl he loves (well, also, Buster Keaton just has that kind of a face).

In this example, the mental imagery we form is clearly aesthetically relevant, so much so that without it the visual joke that follows would not work. Attending to a feature that is represented in mental imagery makes an aesthetic difference. In other words, our aesthetic experience depends heavily on what kind of mental imagery we utilize. And given that the kind of mental imagery we utilize depends on our cultural background, mental imagery is yet another important source of cross-cultural aesthetic variations.

Take the Buster Keaton example again. Suppose someone is unfamiliar with the way jails look. This person is not in a position to form the mental imagery of the jail when seeing the first image of the film. And as a result, this person will miss out on the visual joke of the second shot. This visual joke works only if you have the right kind of mental imagery and you only have the right kind of mental imagery if you come from the right kind of cultural milieu.

Here is another example. Jompet Kuswidananto is a contemporary Indonesian artist. His installations often very explicitly require mental imagery. Take Figure 6.6, for example, where it is not too hard to figure out that we are supposed to form mental imagery of horses. But the kind of mental imagery we form will be very different, depending on our cultural background.

For European or North American observers, the mental imagery of a horse tends to be harmless, maybe even endearing, bringing to mind treasured childhood memories of pony rides. But for observers who grew up in Indonesia, horses are not so harmless as they are associated with soldiers and oppression. So the mental imagery that Indonesians have when looking at this scene will be very different from the mental imagery a European or North American observer would have. And just how this mental imagery unfolds will have a major influence on the aesthetic experience one has of this artwork. Again, imagery is an important source of cross-cultural aesthetic variations.

But aesthetic imagery is important for yet another reason. I have devoted a lot of space to aesthetics in a book on perception. And one may wonder just how close the ties between perception and aesthetics are. True, aesthetics as a discipline was, for centuries, concerned

Figure 6.6 Jompet Kuswidananto: Cortege of the Third Realm, no. 2 (2012). (courtesy of the artist).

with special ways of perceiving. But isn't this connection much less convincing now, when many works at least in the visual arts are not really going for a perceptual effect, but rather a conceptual one? In the age of conceptual art, does it make sense to insist on the close link between aesthetics and perception?

I think that if we take the importance of aesthetic mental imagery seriously, we can see how aesthetics is nonetheless about perceptual phenomena. Remember that mental imagery is perceptual representation that is not directly triggered by sensory input. So it is a form of perceptual representation. And conceptual art – the prime example of non-perceptual art – is in fact, to a great extent, about mental imagery in the sense that the most important aesthetically relevant features are represented by mental imagery. In short, much of conceptual art is a perceptual phenomenon.

Look at this image (Figure 6.7). You may think it's Leonardo's *Mona Lisa*. In fact it is a very different artwork by French conceptual artist Marcel Duchamp from 1965. It is called *L.H.O.O.Q. rasée* (where "rasée" means "shaven"), And the *L.H.O.O.Q.* refers to a much

Figure 6.7 Leonardo da Vinci: Mona Lisa / Marcel Duchamp: L.H.O.O.Q.
Rasée (1965).

earlier artwork by Duchamp from 1919, where Duchamp drew a moustache and beard on the picture of Mona Lisa. You may wonder about the acronym he chose as a title for this. If you pronounce the letters in French, what you get sounds like "Elle a chaud au cul" (my humble translation: "She's horny").

L.H.O.O.Q. rasée is a reference to the earlier picture – but it is perceptually indistinguishable from a faithful reproduction of Leonardo's *Mona Lisa*. But, having seen his moustachioed Mona Lisa, it is very difficult not to see differently from the way we see Leonardo's original.

The missing moustache and beard are very much part of our experience of *L.H.O.O.Q. rasée* – whereas they are not when we look at Leonardo's original. And it is difficult to see how we can describe our experience of *L.H.O.O.Q. rasée* without some reference to the mental imagery of the missing beard and moustache.

The standard story of the art of the 20th century is that artists have gradually turned away from perception and toward concepts. Contemporary art, according to this line of thinking, is not about how things look, but about our ideas. But this is not a convincing story.

Contemporary art is as much about perception as the art of the mid-20th century. But it is largely about a very specific perceptual phenomenon: mental imagery. If we look at some of the most iconic conceptual artworks, it is easy to see that they are not trying to get you to think complex thoughts. They are trying to trigger a specific kind of mental imagery. That is clearly the whole point of *L.H.O.O.Q. rasée*. But there are many other examples.

Here is another famous one: Robert Rauschenberg's *Erased de Kooning drawing* (1953), which is just what it says it is: all we see is an empty piece of paper, with hardly visible traces of the erased drawing on it.

A little background: Willem de Kooning was one of the most influential painters working in New York when the young and not particularly respectful Rauschenberg asked him for a drawing telling him straight up what he was going to do with it. De Kooning did not want to make Rauschenberg's job easier, so he used all kinds of different techniques (pastels, pencils, crayon, charcoal, even ink) to make the erasing less easy.

When you look at the Erased de Kooning drawing, it is difficult not to try to discern what drawing might have been there before Rauschenberg erased it. And this involves trying to conjure up mental imagery of the original drawing.

Susan Sontag was trying to provoke when she wrote, more than 50 years ago: "The basic unit for contemporary art is not the idea, but the analysis of and extension of sensations" (Sontag 1965/1986, p. 300). But the past 50 years have suggested that she was right and we now have a pretty good grip on this "extension of sensation" she talks about: it is about exercising mental imagery.

6.5 THE FREEDOM OF PERCEPTION

At the beginning of the 20th century, Russian formalists had a very distinctive view of aesthetic experiences, one that resonates even today. Their central concept is that of dehabitualization:

> Habitualization devours work, clothes, furniture, one's wife, and the fear of war. [...] And Art exists that one may recover the sensation of life; it exists to make one feel things, to make the stone stony. [...] The technique of art is to make objects 'unfamiliar,' [...] because the process of perception is an aesthetic end in itself and must be prolonged.
>
> (Shklovsky 1917/1965, pp. 11–12)

The general idea is that given the utilitarian nature of perception, we get too used to perceiving certain things around us and become blind to their beauty (Thompson 1988, Nanay 2018c). And aesthetic experience is special because it allows us to see these things with a fresh eye: as if we saw them for the first time.

When we see something for the first time, there are often no practical needs that would determine how we look at this object. Nor are there established patterns of attention, resulting from looking at this thing dozens of times. Our attention is free and open-ended.

Freedom is a tricky concept, but it is also something we all deeply care about. And not just about the freedom to be able to vote, to marry whomever we want to or make decisions about our own body. Even if all these freedoms were granted, as long as our perception is not free, life can be miserable. The freedom of perception is, in some ways, the most basic, but also the most personal form of freedom.

There has been a lot of research on the relation between attention and addiction and one of the clearest behavioral markers of addiction is that the addict's attention is captured very quickly and forcefully by any kind of stimulus that is even remotely related to the addiction (Brevers et al. 2011). So a gambling addict's attention will be captured not only by a photo of a roulette table, but also by a song that was playing last time in the casino or the shirt she once wore in the casino. And in our time, when the attention of even non-addicts is in constant demand by our phones and social media, attention is a precious resource. One very real sense in which addicts are not free is that their perception is not free.

I started this book with an emphasis on what perception is good for and argued at length for the importance of perception in action-guidance. I also made a big deal out of how perception is among the most evolutionarily basic mental states and how we should try to explain the mind starting with simple perceptual states.

But some ways of perceiving are as uniquely human as it gets. What makes aesthetic experience special is that our perception is open-ended and unconstrained (Nanay forthcoming d). There aren't any no-go areas. And this is special because normally our perception is very much constrained by our everyday needs and is in the service of performing various actions. Most of the time, our perception is the opposite of open-ended. But aesthetic experience is different. It sets our perception free. And this freedom, the freedom of perception is among the most human of human capacities.

Perception is special. It is the alpha and the omega of the human mind.

6.6 SUMMARY

Perception in our everyday life is often aimed at helping us to perform actions – this was the topic of Chapter 4. But not always. There are special and precious moments when our perception serves no practical goals – it roams free. This phenomenon has played a crucial role in the discussion of the concept of aesthetic experiences in empirical and philosophical aesthetics.

While there are significant cross-cultural variations in aesthetic experiences, one crucial aspect of all aesthetic experiences is the way attention is exercised. Contemporary psychological and neuroscientific research on the ways in which attention influences our perception can help us understand why aesthetic experiences are special and why we care about them so much.

REFERENCES

Aglioti, S., J. F. X. DeSouza, and M. A. Goodale (1995) Size-contrast illusions deceive the eye but not the hand. *Current Biology* 5: 679–685.

Allen, K. (2015) Hallucination and imagination. *Australasian Journal of Philosophy* 93: 287–302.

Allen, P., F. Larøi, P. K. McGuire, and A. Aleman (2008) The hallucinating brain: a review of structural and functional neuroimaging studies of hallucinations. *Neuroscience and Biobehavioral Reviews* 32(1): 175–191.

Alvarez, G. A., and S. L. Franconeri (2007) How many objects can you track?: Evidence for a resource-limited attentive tracking mechanism. *Journal of Vision* 7: 14.

Bach-y-Rita, P., and S. W. Kercel (2003) Sensory substitution and the human–machine interface. *Trends in Cognitive Sciences* 7: 541–546.

Baird, B., S. LaBerge, and G. Tononi (2021) Two-way communication in lucid REM sleep dreaming. *Trends in Cognitive Sciences* 25: 427–428.

Barnett, K. J., J. J. Foxe, S. Molholm, S. P. Kelly, S. Shalgi, K. J. Mitchell, and F. N. Newell (2008) Differences in early sensory-perceptual processing in synesthesia: a visual evoked potential study. *Neuroimage* 43(3): 605–613.

Batty, C. (2010) Scents and sensibilia. *American Philosophical Quarterly* 47: 103–118.

Baumgarten, A. G. (1758) *Aesthetica*. Frankfurt: J. C. Kleyb.

Bayne, T. (2009) Perception and the reach of phenomenal content. *Philosophical Quarterly* 59: 385–404.

Beck, J. (2018) Marking the perception–cognition boundary: the criterion of stimulus-dependence. *Australasian Journal of Philosophy* 2: 319–334.

Becker, E. S., and M. Rinck (2016) Reversing the mere exposure effect in spider fearfuls. *Biological Psychology* 121: 153–159.

Berger, J., B. Nanay, and J. Quilty-Dunn (2018) Unconscious perceptual justification. *Inquiry* 61: 569–589.

Bergmann, J., E. Genc, A. Kohler, W. Singer, and J. Pearson (2016) Smaller primary visual cortex is associated with stronger, but less precise mental imagery. *Cerebral Cortex* 26: 3838–3850.

Bertelson, P. (1999) Ventriloquism: a case of cross-modal perceptual grouping. In: G. Aschersleben, T. Bachmann, and J. Musseler (eds.), *Cognitive Contributions to the Perception of Spatial and Temporal Events*. Amsterdam: Elsevier, pp. 347–362.

Block, N. (2023) *The Border between Seeing and Thinking*. Oxford: Oxford University Press.

Block, N., and I. Phillips (2016) Debate on unconscious perception. In: B. Nanay (ed.), *Current Controversies in Philosophy of Perception*. New York and London: Routledge, pp. 165–192.

Boas, F. (1927) *Primitive Art*. New York: Dover.

Boduroglu, A., P. Shah, and R. E. Nisbett (2009) Cultural differences in allocation of attention in visual information processing. *Journal of Cross Cultural Psychology* 40: 349–360.

Boghossian, P., and J. Velleman (1989) Colour as a secondary quality. *Mind* 98: 81–103.

Bornstein, R. F. (1989) Exposure and affect: overview and meta-analysis of research, 1967–1987. *Psychological Bulletin* 106: 265–289.

Boroditsky, L., and A. Gaby (2010) Remembrances of times East: absolute spatial representations of time in an Australian Aboriginal community. *Psychological Science* 21: 1635–1639.

Bowker, J. E., and J. K. Sawyers (1988) Influence of exposure on preschoolers' art preferences. *Early Childhood Research Quarterly* 3: 107–115.

Bregman, A. S. (1990) *Auditory Scene Analysis: The Perceptual Organization of Sound*. Cambridge: Bradford Books, MIT.

Brevers, D., A. Cleereman, A. Bechara, C. Lalayaux, C. Kornreich, P. Vebanck, and X. Noel (2011) Time course of attentional bias for gambling information in problem gambling. *Psychology of Addictive Behaviors* 25: 675–682.

Brewer, B. (2011) *Perception and Its Objects*. Oxford: Oxford University Press.

Brewin, C. R. (2014) Episodic memory, perceptual memory, and their interaction: foundations for a theory of posttraumatic stress disorder. *Psychological Bulletin* 140: 69–97.

Briscoe, R. (2018) Superimposed mental imagery: on the uses of make-perceive. In: F. Macpherson, and F. Dorsch (eds.), *Perceptual Memory and Sensory imagination*. Oxford: Oxford University Press, pp. 161–185.

Brogaard, B. (2011) Are there unconscious perceptual processes? *Consciousness and Cognition* 20: 449–463.

Brogaard, B. (2018) In defense of hearing meanings. *Synthese* 195: 2967–2983.

Brown, D. (2018) Infusing perception with imagination. In: F. Macpherson (ed.), *Perceptual Imagination and Perceptual Memory.* Oxford: Oxford University Press, pp. 133–160.

Bullier, J. (2001) Integrated model of visual processing. *Brain Research Reviews* 36: 96–107.

Bullier, J. (2004) Communications between cortical areas of the visual system. In: L. M. Chalupa, and J. S. Werner (eds.), *The Visual Neurosciences.* Cambridge: MIT Press pp. 522–540.

Burch, N. (1973) *Theory of Film Practice.* New York: Praeger.

Burge, T. (2010) *The Origins of Objectivity.* Oxford: Clarendon.

Burton, H. (2003) Visual cortex activity in early and late blind people. *Journal of Neuroscience* 23: 4005–4011.

Busey, T.A., and Parada, F.J. (2010) The nature of expertise in fingerprint examiners. *Psychonomic Bulletin and Review* 17: 155–160.

Camp, E. (2007) Thinking with maps. *Philosophical Perspectives* 21: 145–182.

Campbell, J. (2005) Molyneux's question and cognitive impenetrability. In: A. Raftopoulos (ed.), *Cognitive Penetrabiity of Perception: Attention, Strategies and Bottom-Up Constraints.* New York: Nova Science, pp. 129–139.

Carlino, E, E. Frisaldi, and F. Benedetti (2014) Pain and the context. *Nature Reviews Rheumatology* 10: 348–355.

Cattaneo, Z., and T. Vecchi (2011) *Blind Vision: The Neuroscience of Visual Impairment.* Cambridge: MIT Press.

Cave, K. R., and N. P. Bichot (1999) Visuospatial attention: beyond a spotlight model. *Psychonomic Bulletin and Review* 6: 204–223.

Chua H. F., J. E. Boland, and R. E. Nisbett (2005) Cultural variation in eye movements during scene perception. *Proceedings of the National Academy of Sciences* 102: 12629–12633.

Churchland, P. M. (1981) Eliminative materialism and the propositional attitudes. *Journal of Philosophy* 78: 67–90.

Churchland, P. M. (1988) Folk psychology and the explanation of behavior. *Proceedings of the Aristotelian Society* 62: 209–221.

Clark, A. (2000) *A Theory of Sentience.* Oxford: Clarendon Press.

Cohen, J. (2010) Sounds and temporality. *Oxford Studies in Metaphysics* 5: 303–320.

Coppola, D., and D. Purves (1996) The extraordinarily rapid disappearance of entopic images. *Proceedings of the National Academy of Sciences of the United States of America* 93: 8001–8004.

Crane, T. (2009) Is perception a propositional attitude? *Philosophical Quarterly* 59: 452–469.

Cui, X., C. B. Jeter, D. Yang, P. R. Montague, and D. M. Eagleman (2007) Vividness of mental imagery: individual variability can be measured objectively. *Vision Research* 47: 4474–4478.

Currie, G. (1995) Visual imagery as the simulation of vision. *Mind and Language* 10: 25–44.

de Vignemont, F. (2018) *Mind the Body*. Oxford: Oxford University Press.

Degenaar, M. J. L. (1996) *Molyneux's Problem: Three Centuries of Discussion on the Perception of Forms*. Dordrecht: Kluwer Academic Publishers.

Dehaene, S., L. Naccache, G. Le Clec'H, E. Koechlin, M. Mueller, G. Dehaene-Lambertz, P. F. van de Moortele, and D. Le Bihan (1998) Imaging unconscious semantic priming. *Nature* 395: 597–600.

Dentico, D., B. L. Cheung, J. Y. Chang, J. Guokas, M. Boly, G. Tononi, and B. Van Veen (2014) Reversal of cortical information flow during visual imagery as compared to visual perception. *Neuroimage* 100: 237–243.

Dickie, G. (1964) The myth of aesthetic attitude. *American Philosophical Quarterly* 1: 56–65.

Dijkstra, N., S. E. Bosch, and M. A. J. van Gerven (2019) Shared neural mechanisms of visual perception and imagery. *Trends in Cognitive Sciences* 23: 423–434.

Dodsworth, C., L. J. Norman, and L. Thaler (2020) Navigation and perception of spatial layout in virtual echo-acoustic space. *Cognition* 197: 104185.

Döring, S. A. (2007) Seeing what to do: affective perception and rational motivation. *Dialectica* 61: 363–394.

Douglas, R. J., and Martin, K. A. (2007) Mapping the matrix: the ways of neocortex. *Neuron* 56(2): 226–238.

Dretske, F. (1986) Misrepresentation. In: R. Bogdan (ed.), *Belief*. Oxford: Oxford University Press, pp. 17–36.

Dretske, F. 1988 *Explaining Behavior. Reasons in a World of Causes*. Cambridge: The MIT Press.

Dugue, L., E. P. Merriam, D. J. Heeger, and M. Carrasco (2020) Differential impact of endogenous and exogenous attention on activity in human visual cortex. *Scientific Reports* 10: 21274.

Dunham, Y., A. S. Baron, and M. R. Banaji (2008) The development of implicit intergroup cognition. *Trends in Cognitive Sciences* 12: 248–253.

Dupré, J. (1981) Natural kinds and biological taxa. *The Philosophical Review* 90: 66–90.

Ekroll, V., B. Sayim, R. Van der Hallen, and J. Wagemans (2016) Illusory visual completion of an object's invisible backside can make your finger feel shorter. *Current Biology* 26: 1029–1033.

Elkin, J. (ed.) (2006) *Is Art History Global?* London: Routledge.

Evans, G. (1985) Molyneux's question. In: A. Phillips (ed.), *Gareth Evans: Collected Papers*. Oxford: Clarendon Press.

Evans, K. K., D. Georgian-Smith, R. Tambouret, R. L. Birdwell, and J. M. Wolfe (2013) The gist of the abnormal: above-chance medical decision making in the blink of an eye. *Psychonomic Bulletin & Review* 20(6): 1170–1175.

Fairhurst, M. T., E. Travers, V. Hayward, and O. Deroy (2018) Confidence is higher in touch than in vision in cases of perceptual ambiguity. *Scientific Reports* 8: 15604.

Fazekas, P., and B. Nanay (2021) Attention is amplification, not selection. *British Journal for the Philosophy of Science* 72: 299–324.

Fazekas, P., B. Nanay, and J. Pearson (2021) Offline perception. Special issue of *Philosophical Transaction of the Royal Society B* 376(1817): 20190686.

Fazekas, P., G. Nemeth, and M. Overgaard (2019) White dreams are made of colours: what studying contentless dreams can teach about the neural basis of dreaming and conscious experiences. *Sleep Medicine Reviews* 43: 84–91.

Findlay, J. M., and I. D. Gilchrist (2003) *Active Vision: The Psychology of Looking and Seeing*. Oxford: Oxford University Press.

Firestone, C., and B. J. Scholl (2016) Cognition does not affect perception. *Behavioral and Brain Sciences* 39: 1–72.

Fodor, J. A. (1983) *The Modularity of Mind*. Cambridge: The MIT Press.

Franz, V., and K. Gegenfurtner (2008) Grasping visual illusions: consistent data and no dissociation. *Cognitive Neuropsychology* 25: 920–950.

Franz, V., K. Gegenfurtner, H. Bülthoff, and M. Fahle (2000) Grasping visual illusions: no evidence for a dissociation between perception and action. *Psychological Science* 11: 20–25.

French, C. (2018) Naïve realism and diaphaneity. *Proceedings of the Aristotelian Society* 118: 149–175.

Friston K. (2010) The free-energy principle: a unified brain theory? *Nature Review Neuroscience* 11: 127–138.

Frith C. D., and D. J. Done (1988) Towards a neuropsychology of schizophrenia. *British Journal of Psychiatry* 153: 437–443.

Fulkerson, M. (2014) *The First Sense: A Philosophical Study of Human Touch*. Cambridge: The MIT Press.

Funkhouser, E. (2006) The determinable-determinate relation. *Nous* 40: 548–569.

Gandhi, S. P., D. J. Heeger and G. M. Boynton (1999) Spatial attention affects brain activity in human primary visual cortex. *Proceedings of the National Academy of Sciences* 96 (1999): 3314–3319.

Girard, P., J. M. Hupe, and J. Bullier (2001) Feedforward and feedback connections between areas V1 and V2 of the monkey have similar conduction velocities. *Journal of Neurophysiology* 85: 1328–1331.

Godfrey-Smith, P. (2020) *Metazoa*. New York: Macmillan.

Goh, J. O., M. W. Chee, J. C. Tan, V. Venkatraman, A. Hebrank, E. D. Leshikar, L. Jenkins, B. P. Sutton, A. H. Gutchess and D. C. Park (2007) Age and culture modulate object processing and object-scene binding in the ventral visual area. *Cognitive, Affective, and Behavioral Neuroscience* 7: 44–52.

Goldman, A. (1999) *Knowledge in a Social World*. Oxford: Clarendon Press.

Gonzalez, R. (2013) Wine tasting is bullshit. Here's why. *Gizmondo*. https://gizmodo.com/wine-tasting-is-bullshit-heres-why-496098276.

Goodale, M. A., and A. D. Milner (2004) *Sights Unseen*. Oxford: Oxford University Press.

Goodale, M. A., D. Pelisson, and C. Prablanc (1986) Large adjustments in visually guided reaching do not depend on vision of the hand or perception of target displacement. *Nature* 320: 748–750.

Green, E. J. (2022) Representing shape in sight and touch. *Mind & Language* 37: 694–714.

Grice, H. P. (1962) Some remarks about the senses. In: R. J. Butler (ed.), *Analytical Philosophy*. Oxford: Basil Blackwell, pp. 133–153.

Grill-Spector, K., and R. Malach (2004) The human visual cortex. *Annual Review of Neuroscience* 27: 649–677.

Gruters, K. G., D. L. K. Murphy, C. D. Jenson, D. W. Smith, C. A. Shera, and J. M. Groh (2018) The eardrums move when the eyes move: a multisensory effect on the mechanics of hearing. *Proceedings of the National Academy of Science* 115(6): E1309–E1318.

Gutteling, T. P., N. Petridou, S. O. Dumoulin, B. M. Harvey, E. J. Aarnoutse, J. Leon Kenemans, and S. F. W. Neggers (2015) Action preparation shapes processing in early visual cortex. *The Journal of Neuroscience* 35: 6472–6480.

Hare, B., J. Call, B. Agnetta, and M. Tomasello (2000) Chimpanzees know what conspecifics do and do not see. *Animal Behavior* 59: 771–785.

Harrison, J., and S. Baron-Cohen (1997) Synesthesia: a review of psychological theory. In: S. Baron-Cohen, and J. E. Harrison (eds.), *Synaesthesia: Classic and Contemporary Readings*. Oxford: Basil Blackwell, pp. 109–122.

Held, R., Y. Ostrovsky, T. Gandhi, S. Ganesh, U. Mathur, and P. Sinha (2011) The newly sighted fail to match seen with felt. *Nature Neuroscience* 14(5): 551–553.

Helton, G., and B. Nanay (2019) Amodal completion and knowledge. *Analysis* 79: 415–423.

Helton, G., and B. Nanay (2023) Against the very idea of perceptual beliefs. *Analytic Philosophy*, 64: 93–105.

Henkin, R. I., L. M. Levy, and C. S. Lin (2000) Taste and smell phantoms revealed by brain functional MRI (fMRI). *Journal of Computer Assisted Tomography* 24(1): 106–123.

Hobbes, T. (1655) *De Corpore*. London: J. Bohn.

Hohwy, J. (2013) *The Predictive Mind*. New York: Oxford University Press.

Horikawa, T., and Y. Kamitani (2017) Hierarchical neural representation of dreamed objects revealed by brain decoding with deep neural network features. *Frontiers Computational Neuroscience* 11: 4. doi: 10.3389/fncom.2017.00004.

Hubbard, E. M., A. Cyrus Arman, V. S. Ramachandran, and G. M. Boynton (2005) Individual differences among grapheme-color synesthetes: brain-behavior correlations. *Neuron* 45(6): 975–985.

Hummel, T., J. F. Delwiche, C. Schmidt, and K.-B. Hutterbrink (2003) Effects of the form of glasses on the perception of wine flavors. *Appetite* 41: 197–202.

Hung, S.-M., and P.-J. Hsieh (2022) Mind wandering in sensory cortices. *Neuroimage: Reports* 2: 100073.

Jackson, F. (1977) *Perception: A Representative Theory*. Cambridge: Cambridge University Press.

James, W. (1890) *The Principles of Psychology, in Two Volumes*. New York: Henry Holt & Co.

Jarodzka, H., K. Schieter, P. Gerjets, and T. van Gog (2010) In the eyes of the beholder: how experts and novices interpret dynamic stimuli. *Learning and Instruction* 20: 146–154.

Jeannerod, M. (1997) *The Cognitive Neuroscience of Action*. Oxford: Blackwell.

Ji, L. J., K. Peng, and R. E. Nisbett (2000) Culture, control and perception of relationships in the environment. *Journal of Personality and Social Psychology* 78: 943–955.

Jiang, Y., P. Costello, F. Fang, M. Huang, and S. He (2006) A gender- and sexual orientation-dependent spatial attentional effect of invisible images. *PNAS* 103(45): 17048–17052.

Jonas, C. N., A. J. G. Taylor, S. Hutton, P. H. Weiss, and J. Ward (2011) Visuospatial representations of the alphabet in synaesthetes and non-synaesthetes. *Journal of Neuropsychology* 5(2): 302–322.

Jones, C. L., M. A. Gray, L. Minati, J. Simner, H. D. Critchley, and J. Ward (2011) The neural basis of illusory gustatory sensations: two rare cases of lexicalgustatory synaesthesia. *Journal of Neuropsychology* 5(2): 243–254.

Judge, J., and B. Nanay (2021) Expectations. In: N. Nielsen, J. Levinson, and T. McAuley (eds.), *Oxford Handbook of Music and Philosophy*. New York: Oxford University Press, pp. 997–1018.

Kaas, J. H., and T. A. Hackett (1999) "What" and "where" processing in auditory cortex. *Nature Neuroscience* 2: 1045–1047.

Kant, I. (1790/1928) *Critique of Judgment*. Oxford: Oxford University Press.

Katzner, S., and S. Weigelt (2013) Visual cortical networks: of mice and men. *Current Opinion in Neurobiology* 23: 202–206.

Kavanagh, D. J., J. Andrade, and J. May (2005) Imaginary relish and exquisite torture: the elaborated intrusion theory of desire. *Psychological Review* 112(2): 446–467.

Kentridge, R. W., C. A. Heywood, and L. Weiskrantz (1999) Attention without awareness in blindsight. *Proceedings of the Royal Society of London. Series B* 266: 1805–1811.

Kind, A. (2017) Imaginative vividness. *Journal of the American Philosophical Association* 3: 32–50.

Koenig-Robert, R., and J. Pearson (2020) Decoding non-conscious thought representations during successful thought suppression. *Journal of Cognitive Neuroscience* 32: 2272–2284.

Kok, P., L. J. Bains, T. Van Mourik, D. G. Norris, and F. P. de Lange (2016) Selective activation of the deep layers of the human primary visual cortex by top-down feedback. *Current Biology* 26: 371–376.

Kok, P., M. F. Failing, and F. P. de Lange (2014) Prior expectations evoke stimulus templates in the primary visual cortex. *Journal of Cognitive Neuroscience* 26: 1546–1554.

Kompus, K., L. E. Falkenberg, J. J. Bless, E. Johnsen, R. A. Kroken, B. Krakvik, F. Laroi, E.-M. Loberg, E. Vedul-Kjelsas, R. Westerhausen, and K. Hugdahl (2013) The role of the primary auditory cortex in the neural mechanism of auditory verbal hallucinations. *Frontiers in Human Neuroscience*. 10.3389/fnhum.2013.00144.

Kompus, K., R. Westerhausen, and K. Hugdahl (2011) The 'paradoxical' engagement of the primary auditory cortex in patients with auditory verbal hallucinations: a meta-analysis of functional neuroimaging studies. *Neuropsychologia* 49: 3361–3369.

Konkoly, K. R., K. Appel, E. Chabani, A. Manguaruga, J. Gott, R. Mallett, B. Caughran, S. Witkowski, N. W. Whitmore, C. Y. Mazurek, J. B. Berent, F. D. Weber, B. Turker, S. Leu-Semenescu, J-B. Maranci, G. Pipa, I. Arnulf, D. Oudiette, M. Dresler, and K. A. Paller (2021) Real-time dialogue between experimenters and dreamers during REM sleep. *Current Biology* 31: 1417–1427.

Kosslyn, S. M., M. Behrmann, and M. Jeannerod (1995) The cognitive neuroscience of mental imagery. *Neuropsychologia* 33: 1335–1344.

Kouider, S., and S. Dehaene (2007) Levels of processing during non-conscious perception: a critical review of visual masking. *Philosophical Transactions of the Royal Society B* 362: 857–875.

Kowler, E., E. Anderson, B. Dosher, and E. Blaser (1995) The role of attention in the programming of saccades. *Vision Research* 35: 1897–1916.

Kulvicki, J. (2008) The nature of noise. *Philosophers' Imprint* 8: 1–16.

Kulvicki, J. (2014) *Images*. London: Routledge.

LaBerge, S., B. Baird, and P. G. Zimbardo (2018) Smooth tracking of visual targets distinguishes lucid REM sleep dreaming and waking perception from imagination. *Nature Communications* 9: 3298.

Lackey, J. (2006) Knowing from testimony. *Philosophy Compass* 1: 432–448.

Laeng, B., I. M. Bloem, S. D'Ascenzo, and L. Tommasi (2014) Scrutinizing visual images: the role of gaze in mental imagery and memory. *Cognition* 131: 263–283.

Lebrecht, S., M. Bar, L. F. Barrett, and M. J. Tarr (2012) Micro-valences: perceiving affective valence in everyday objects. *Frontiers in Psychology* 3:107. doi: 10.3389/fpsyg.2012.00107.

Leddington, J. P. (2019) Sounds fully simplified. *Analysis* 79(4): 621–629.

Lee, T. S., and M. Nguyen (2001) Dynamics of subjective contour formation in the early visual cortex. *Proceedings of the National Academy of Sciences* 98: 1907–1911.

Levin, J. (2008) Molyneux's question and the individuation of perceptual concepts. *Philosophical Studies* 139: 1–28.

Linscott, R. J., and J. van Os (2013) An updated and conservative systematic review and meta-analysis of epidemiological evidence on psychotic experiences in children and adults: on the pathway from proneness to persistence to dimensional expression across mental disorders. *Psychological Medicine* 43: 1133–1149.

Logue, H. (2012) Why naive realism? *Proceedings of the Aristotelian Society* 112(2pt2): 211–237.

Lopes, D. M. (1996) *Understanding Pictures.* Oxford: Oxford University Press.

Lopes, D. M., S. Matherne, M. Matthen, and B. Nanay (2024) *The Geography of Taste.* New York: Oxford University Press.

Lopes, D. M., B. Nanay, and N. Riggle (2021) *Aesthetic Life and Why It Matters.* New York: Oxford University Press.

Lupyan, G. (2015) Cognitive penetrability of perception in the age of prediction: predictive systems are penetrable systems. *Review of Philosophy and Psychology* 6(4): 547–569.

Lycan, W. (2000) The slighting of smell. In: N. Bhushan, and S. Rosenfeld (eds), *Of Minds and Molecules: New Philosophical Perspectives on Chemistry.* Oxford: Oxford University Press, pp. 273–289.

Lyons, J. (2009) *Perception and Basic Beliefs.* New York: Oxford University Press.

Mack, A. (2002) Is the visual world a grand illusion? *Journal of Consciousness Studies* 9: 102–110.

Mack, A., and I. Rock (1998) *Inattentional Blindness.* Cambridge: MIT Press.

Macpherson, F. (2014) The space of sensory modalities. In: D. Stokes, M. Matthen, and S. Biggs (eds.), *Perception and Its Modalities.* Oxford: Oxford University Press, pp. 432–461.

Maier, M., and R. A. Rahman (2018) Native language promotes access to visual consciousness. *Psychological Science* 29: 1757–1772.

Mainland, J., and N. Sobel (2006) The sniff is part of the olfactory percept. *Chemical Senses* 31: 181–196.

Manescu, S., J. Frasnelli, F. Lepore and J. Djordjevic (2014) Now you like me, now you don't: Impact of labels on odor perception. *Chemical Senses* 39: 167–175.

Markus, H., and S. Kitayama (1991) Culture and the self: implications for cognition, emotion and motivation. *Psychological Review* 98: 224–253.

Martinez, M., and B. Nanay (forthcoming) Many-to-one intentionalism. *Journal of Philosophy*, forthcoming.

Mast, F. W., and Kosslyn, S. M. (2002) Eye movements during visual mental imagery. *Trends in Cognitive Science* 6: 271–272.

Masuda, T., and R. E. Nisbett (2001) Attending holistically versus analytically: comparing the context sensitivity of Japanese and Americans. *Journal of Personality and Social Psychology* 81: 922–934.

Matthen, M. (2014) Active perception and the representation of space. In: D. Stokes, M. Matthen, and S. Biggs (eds.), *Perception and Its Modalities*. Oxford: Oxford University Press, pp. 44–72.

Matthen, M. (2021) Dual structure of touch: the body vs. peripersonal space. In: F. de Vignemont (ed.), *The World at Our Fingertips*. Oxford University Press, pp. 197–214.

Matthen, M., and J. Cohen (2020) Many Molyneux questions. *Australasian Journal of Philosophy* 98: 47–63.

Mechelli, A., C. J. Price, K. J. Friston, and A. Ishai (2004) Where bottom-up meets top-down: neuronal interactions during perception and imagery. *Cerebral Cortex* 14: 1256–1265.

Meyer, L. B. (1956) *Emotion and Meaning in Music*. Chicago, IL: University of Chicago Press.

Michotte, A., and L. Burke (1951) Une nouvelle énigme de la psychologie de la perception: le "donnée amodal" dans l'experience sensorielle. *Actes du XIII Congrés Internationale de Psychologie*, Stockholm, Proceedings and Papers, pp. 179–180.

Millikan, R. G. (1984) *Language, Thought and Other Biological Categories*. Cambridge: The MIT Press.

Miyamoto, Y., R. E. Nisbett, and T. Masuda (2006) Differential affordances of Eastern and Western environments. *Psychological Science* 17(2): 113–119.

Morrison, J. (2016) Perceptual confidence. *Analytic Philosophy* 57(1): 15–48.

Morrot, G., F. Brochet, and D. Dubourdieu (2001) The color of odors. *Brain and Language* 79: 309–320.

Munton, J. (2017) Visual confidences and direct perceptual justification. *Philosophical Topics* 44(2): 301–326.

Murphy, G. (1956) Affects and perceptual learning. *Psychological Review* 63(1): 1–15.

Murphy, M. C., A. C. Nau, C. Fisher, S. G. Kim, J. S. Schuman, and K. C. Chan (2016) Top-down influence on the visual cortex of the blind during sensory substitution. *Neuroimage* 125: 932–940.

Murray, S. O., D. Kersten, B. A. Olshausen, P. Schrater, and D. L. Woods (2002) Shape perception reduces activity in human primary visual cortex. *PNAS* 99: 15164–15169.

Nanay, B. (2006) Does what we want influence what we see? In: R. Sun (ed.), *Proceedings of the 28th Annual Conference of the Cognitive Science Society (CogSci 2006)*. Hillsdale, NJ: Lawrence Erlbaum, pp. 615–621.

Nanay, B. (2008) Picture perception and the two visual subsystems. In: B. C. Love, K. McRae, and V. M. Sloutsky (eds.), *Proceedings of the 30th Annual Conference of the Cognitive Science Society (CogSci 2008)*. Hillsdale, NJ: Lawrence Erlbaum, 2008, pp. 975–980.

Nanay, B. (2010a) Attention and perceptual content. *Analysis* 70: 263–270.

Nanay, B. (2010b) Perception and Imagination: amodal perception as mental imagery. *Philosophical Studies* 150: 239–254.

Nanay, B. (2010c) A modal theory of function. *Journal of Philosophy* 107: 412–431.

Nanay, B. (2011a) Do we see apples as edible? *Pacific Philosophical Quarterly* 92: 305–322.

Nanay, B. (2011b) Do we sense modalities with our sense modalities? *Ratio* 24: 299–310.

Nanay, B. (2011c) Ambiguous pictures, attention and perceptual content. *Phenomenology and the Cognitive Sciences* 10: 557–561.

Nanay, B. (2011d) Perceiving pictures. *Phenomenology and the Cognitive Sciences* 10: 461–480.

Nanay, B. (2012a) Perceptual phenomenology. *Philosophical Perspectives* 26: 235–246.

Nanay, B. (2012b) Action-oriented perception. *European Journal of Philosophy* 20: 430–446.

Nanay, B. (2013) *Between Perception and Action*. Oxford: Oxford University Press.

Nanay, B. (2014) Empirical problems with anti-representationalism. In: B. Brogaard (ed.), *Does Perception Have Content?* New York: Oxford University Press, pp. 39–50.

Nanay, B. (2015a) Perceptual content and the content of mental imagery. *Philosophical Studies* 172: 1723–1736.

Nanay, B. (2015b) Aesthetic attention. *Journal of Consciousness Studies* 22(5–6): 96–118.

Nanay, B. (2015c) *Trompe l'oeil* and the dorsal/ventral account of picture perception. *Review of Philosophy and Psychology* 6: 181–197.

Nanay, B. (2016a) Hallucination as mental imagery. *Journal of Consciousness Studies* 23(7–8): 65–81.

Nanay, B. (2016b) The role of imagination in decision-making. *Mind & Language* 31: 126–142.

Nanay, B. (2016c) *Aesthetics as Philosophy of Perception*. Oxford: Oxford University Press.

Nanay, B. (2017) Sensory substitution and multimodal mental imagery. *Perception* 46: 1014–1026.

Nanay, B. (2018a) Multimodal mental imagery. *Cortex* 105: 125–134.

Nanay, B. (2018b) The importance of amodal completion in everyday perception. *i-Perception* 9(4): 1–16. doi: 10.1177/204166951878887.

Nanay, B. (2018c) Defamiliarization and the unprompted (not innocent) eye. *Nonsite* 24: 1–17.

Nanay, B. (2018d) Threefoldness. *Philosophical Studies* 175: 163–182.

Nanay, B. (2019) *Aesthetics: A Very Short Introduction*. Oxford: Oxford University Press.

Nanay, B. (2020a) Vicarious representation: a new theory of social cognition. *Cognition* 205: 104451.

Nanay, B. (2020b) Molyneux's question and interpersonal variations in multimodal mental imagery among blind subjects. In: G. Ferretti, and B. Glenney (eds.), *Molyneux's Question and the History of Philosophy*. London: Routledge, pp. 257–263.

Nanay, B. (2020c) Perceiving indeterminately. *Thought* 9: 160–166.

Nanay, B. (2021a) Unconscious mental imagery. *Philosophical Transactions of the Royal Society B* 376(1817): 20190689.

Nanay, B. (2021b) Synesthesia as (multimodal) mental imagery. *Multisensory Research* 34: 281–296.

Nanay, B. (2022a) Entity realism about mental representations. *Erkenntnis* 87: 75–91.

Nanay, B. (2022b) The sensory individuals of picture perception. *Philosophical Studies* 179: 3729–3746.

Nanay, B. (2022c) Amodal completion and relationalism. *Philosophical Studies* 179: 2537–2551.

Nanay, B. (2022d) Going global: A cautiously optimistic manifesto. *Contemporary Aesthetics*, Special Volume 10: 3.

Nanay, B. (2023) *Mental Imagery*. Oxford: Oxford University Press.

Nanay, B. (forthcoming a) The selective advantage of representing correctly. *Philosophy and Phenomenological Research*, forthcoming.

Nanay, B. (forthcoming b) *Global Aesthetics*. Oxford: Oxford University Press.

Nanay, B. (forthcoming c) Franz Boas and the primacy of form. *British Journal of Aesthetics*, forthcoming.

Nanay, B. (forthcoming d) Aesthetic experience as interaction. *Journal of the American Philosophical Association*, forthcoming.

Nanay, B. (forthcoming e) Perception and mental imagery in our engagement with art. In: A. King (ed.), *Art and Philosophy*. Oxford: Oxford University Press, forthcoming.

Nisbett, R. E. (2003) *The Geography of Thought: How Asians and Westerners Think Differently … And Why*. New York: Free Press.

Nisbett, R. E., K. Peng, I. Choi, and A. Norenzayan (2001) Culture and systems of thought: holistic vs. analytic cognition. *Psychological Review* 108: 291–310.

Norman, L. J., and L. Thaler (2019) Retinotopic-like maps of spatial sound in primary 'visual' cortex of blind human echolocators. *Proceedings of the Royal Society B* 286: 20191910.

Nudds, M. (2010) What are auditory objects? *Review of Philosophy and Psychology* 1: 105–122.

Núñez, R. E., and E. Sweetser (2006) With the future behind them: convergent evidence from Aymara language and gesture in the crosslinguistic comparison of spatial construals of time. *Cognitive Science* 30: 401–450.

Nunn, J. A., L. J. Gregory, M. J. Brammer, S. C. Williams, D. M. Parslow, M. J. Morgan, R. G. Morris, E. T. Bullmore, S. Baron-Cohen, and J. A. Gray (2002) Functional magnetic resonance imaging of synesthesia: activation of V4/V8 by spoken words. *Nature Neuroscience* 5(4): 371–375.

O'Callaghan, C. (2007) *Sounds*. Oxford: Oxford University Press.

O'Callaghan, C. (2008) Seeing what you hear: cross-modal illusions and perception. *Philosophical Issues* 18(1): 316–338.

O'Connor, D. H., M. M. Fukui, M. A. Pinsk, and S. Kastner (2002) Attention modulates responses in the human lateral geniculate nucleus. *Nature Neuroscience* 5(11): 1203–1209.

Orlandi, N. (2014) *The Innocent Eye*. New York: Oxford University Press.

Paulignan, Y., C. L. MacKenzie, R. G. Marteniuk, and M. Jeannerod (1991) Selective perturbation of visual input during prehension movements: 1. The effect of changing object position. *Experimental Brain Research* 83: 502–512.

Pautz, A. (2010) An argument for the intentional view of visual experience. In: Nanay, B. (ed.), *Perceiving the World*. Oxford: Oxford University Press, pp. 254–309.

Pearson, J., T. Naselaris, E. A. Holmes, and S. M. Kosslyn (2015) Mental imagery: functional mechanisms and clinical applications. *Trends in Cognitive Sciences* 19: 590–602.

Peerdeman, K. J., A. I. van Laarhoven, S. M. Keij, L. Vase, M. M. Rovers, M. L. Peters, and A. W. Evers (2016) Relieving patients' pain with expectation interventions: a meta-analysis. *Pain* 157: 1179–1191.

Pekkola, J., V. Ojanen, T. Autti, I. P. Jaaskelainen, R. Mottonen, A. Tarkainen, and M. Sams (2005) Primary auditory cortex activation by visual speech: an fMRI study at 3 T. *NeuroReport* 16: 125–128.

Pelisson, D., C. Prablanc, M. A. Goodale, and M. Jeannerod (1986) Visual control of reaching movements without vision of the limb: II. Evidence of fast unconscious processes correcting the trajectory of the hand to the final position of a double-step stimulus. *Experimental Brain Research* 62: 303–311.

Phillips, I. (2011) Indiscriminability and experience of change. *The Philosophical Quarterly* 61(245): 808–827.

Phillips, I. (2014) Lack of imagination: individual differences in mental imagery and the significance of consciousness. In: , J. Kallestrup, and M. Sprevak (eds.), *New Waves in Philosophy of Mind*. London: Palgrave Macmillan, pp. 278–300.

Phillips, B. (2019) The shifting border between perception and cognition. *Noûs* 53(2): 316–346.

Piaget, J. (1928) *The Child's Conception of the World*. London: Routledge and Kegan Paul.

Ploghaus, A., L. Becerra, C. Borras, and D. Borsook (2003) Neural circuitry underlying pain modulation: expectation, hypnosis, placebo. *Trends in Cognitive Sciences* 7: 197–200.

Porter, J., B. Craven, R. Khan, S.-J. Chang, I. Kang, B. Judkewitz, and N. Sobel (2007) Mechanisms of scent tracking in humans. *Nature Neuroscience* 10: 27–29.

Posner, M. I. (1980) Orienting of attention. *Quaterly Journal of Experimental Psychology* 32: 2–25.

Posner, M. I., J. A. Walker, F. J. Friedrich, and R. D. Rafal (1984) Effects of parietal injury on covert orienting of attention. *Journal of Neuroscience* 4: 1863–1874.

Pryor, J. (2000) The skeptic and the dogmatist. *Noûs* 34(4): 517–549.

Pylyshyn, Z. (1999) Is vision continuous with cognition?: The case for cognitive impenetrability of visual perception. *Behavioral and Brain Sciences* 22: 341–365.

Qiu, F. T., and R. von der Heydt (2005) Figure and ground in the visual cortex: V2 combines stereoscopic cues with gestalt rules. *Neuron* 47: 155–166.

Quilty-Dunn, J. (2020) Perceptual pluralism. *Noûs* 54: 807–838.

Reed, C. L., R. L. Klatzky, and E. Halgren (2005) What vs. where in touch: an fMRI study. *NeuroImage* 25: 718–726.

Rees, G., C. Russell, C. D. Firth, and J. Driver (1999) Inattentional blindness versus inattentional amnesia for fixated but ignored words. *Science* 286: 2504–2507.

Reisberg, D., D. G. Pearson, and S. M. Kosslyn (2003) Intuitions and introspections about imagery: the role of imagery experience in shaping an investigator's theoretical views. *Journal of Applied Psychology* 17: 147–160.

Roelfsema, P. R., and F. P. de Lange (2016) Eary visual cortex as a multiscale cognitive blackboard. *Annual Review of Visual Science* 2: 131–151.

Rubenstein, A. J., L. Kalakanis, and J. H. Langlois (1999) Infant preferences for attractive faces: a cognitive explanation. *Developmental Psychology* 15: 848–855.

Sagiv, N., J. Heer, and L. Robertson (2006) Does binding of synesthetic color to the evoking grapheme require attention? *Cortex* 42 (2): 232–242.

Schellenberg, S. (2010) Particularity and phenomenology of perceptual experience. *Philosophical Studies* 149: 19–48.

Schenk, T., and R. D. McIntosh (2010) Do we have independent visual streams for perception and action? *Cognitive Neuroscience* 1: 52–78.

Schwitzgebel, E. (2008) The unreliability of naive introspection. *Philosophical Review* 117: 245–273.

Seli, P., M. J. Kane, J. Smallwood, D. L. Schacter, D. Maillet, J. W. Schooler, and D. Smilek (2018) Mind-wandering as a natural kind: a family-resemblances view. *Trends in Cognitive Sciences* 22: 479–490.

Shams, L., Y. Kamitani, and S. Shimojo (2000) What you see is what you hear. *Nature* 408: 788.

Shea, N. (2018) *Representation in Cognitive Science*. Oxford: Oxford University Press.

Shklovsky, V. (1917/1965) Art as technique. In: L.T. Lemon, and M.J. Reis (eds.), *Russian Formalist Criticism: Four Essays*. Lincoln: University of Nebraska Press, pp. 3–24.

Siclari, J. L., B. Postle, and G. Tononi (2013) Assessing sleep consciousness within subjects using a serial awakening paradigm. *Frontiers in Psychology* 4: 542.

Siegel, S. (2006) Which properties are represented in perception? In T. Gendler, and J. Hawthorne (eds.), *Perceptual Experience*. Oxford: Oxford University Press, pp. 481–503.

Simmons, D. J., and C. F. Chabris (1999) Gorillas in our midst: sustained inattentional blindness for dynamic events. *Perception* 28: 1059–1074.

Simner, J. (2012) Defining synaesthesia. *British Journal of Psychology* 103: 1–15.

Smith, B. (2009) Speech sounds and the direct meeting of minds. In: M. Nudds, and C. O'Callaghan (eds.), *Sounds and Perception*. Oxford: Oxford University Press, pp. 183–210.

Smith, B. C. (2012) Perspective: complexities of flavour. *Nature* 486: S6.

Southgate, V. (2020) Are infants altercentric? The other and the self in early social cognition. *Psychological Review* 127: 505–523.

Spence, C. (2015) Eating with our ears: assessing the importance of the sounds of consumption on our perception and enjoyment of multisensory flavour experiences. *Flavour* 4: 3.

Spence, C., M. Auvray, and B. C. Smith (2014) Confusing tastes with flavours. In: D. Stokes, M. Matthen, & S. Biggs (eds.), *Perception and Its Modalities*. Oxford: Oxford University Press, pp. 247–274.

Stazicker, J. (2011) Attention, visual consciousness and indeterminacy. *Mind & Language* 26(2): 156–184.

Sterzer, P., J.-D. Haynes, and G. Rees (2006) Primary visual cortex activation on the path of apparent motion is mediated by feedback from hMT+/V5. *NeuroImage* 32(3): 1308–1316.

Stich, S. P. (1983) *From Folk Psychology to Cognitive Science: The Case against Belief*. Oxford: Oxford University Press.

Stich, S. P. (1996) *Deconstructing the Mind*. Oxford: Oxford University Press.

Stokes, D. (2012) Perceiving and desiring: a new look at the cognitive penetrability of experience. *Philosophical Studies* 158: 479–492.

Stokes, D. (2021) *Thinking and Perceiving: On the Malleability of the Mind*. London: Routledge.

Stokes, D., and B. Nanay (2020) Perceptual skills. In: E. Fridland, and C. Pavese (eds.), *Routledge Handbook of the Philosophy of Skill and Expertise*. London: Routledge, pp. 314–323.

Stolnitz, J. (1960) *Aesthetics and Philosophy of Art Criticism*. New York: Houghton Mifflin.

Sontag, S. (1965/1986) One culture and the new sensibility. In: S. Sontag (ed.), *Against Interpretation*. New York: Farrar Straus Giroux, pp. 293–304.

Tang, J., J. Ward, and B. Butterworth (2008) Number forms in the brain. *Journal of Cognitive Neuroscience* 20(9): 1547–1556.

Teufel, C., S. C. Dakin, and P. C. Fletcher (2018) Prior object-knowledge sharpens properties of early visual feature-detectors. *Scientific Reports* 8: 10853.

Teufel, C., and B. Nanay (2017) How to (and how not to) think about top-down influences on perception. *Consciousness and Cognition* 47: 17–25.

Thielen, J., S. E. Bosch, T. M. van Leeuwen, M. A. van Gerven, and R. van Lier (2019) Neuroimaging findings on amodal completion: a review. *i-Perception* 10(2): 2041669519840047.

Thompson, K. (1988) *Breaking the Glass Armor*. Neoformalist Film Analysis. Princeton, NJ: Princeton University Press.

Thoreson, W. B., N. Babai, and T. M. Bartoletti (2008) Feedback from horizontal cells to rod photoreceptors in vertebrate retina. *The Journal of Neuroscience* 28: 5691–5695.

Toole, A. J., and N. Fogd (2021) Head and eye movements and gaze tracking in baseball batting. *Optometry and Vision Science* 98: 750–758.

Tritsch, M. F. (1990) Temperature sensation: the "3-bowls experiment" revisited. *Naturwissenschaften* 77(6): 288–289. doi: 10.1007/BF01131227.

Van Essen, D. C. (2004) Organization of visual areas in macaque and human cerebral cortex. In: L. Chalupa, and J. S. Werner (eds.), *The Visual Neurosciences*. Cambridge: MIT Press, pp. 507–521.

Van Leeuwen, N. (2011) Imagination is where the action is. *Journal of Philosophy* 108: 55–77.

Van Westen, A. (2022) The philosophy of temperature perception. PhD dissertation, University of Antwerp.

VandenBos, G. R. (2007) *American Psychological Association: Dictionary of Psychology*. New York: Psychology Press.

Vetter, P., and A. Newen (2014) Varieties of cognitive penetration in visual perception. *Consciousness & Cognition* 27: 62–75.

Vetter, P., F. W. Smith, and L. Muckli (2014) Decoding sound and imagery content in early visual cortex. *Current Biology* 24: 1256–1262.

Villey, P. (1930) *The World of the Blind*. Oxford: Macmillan.

Von der Heydt, R., and N. R. Zhang (2018) Figure and ground: how the visual cortex integrates local cues for global organization. *Journal of Neurophysiology* 120: 3085–3098.

Voss, U., K. Schermelleh-Engel, J. Windt, C. Frenzel, and A. Hobson (2013) Measuring consciousness in dreams: the lucidity and consciousness in dreams scale. *Consciousness and Cognition* 22: 8–21.

Walton, K. (1990) *Mimes Is as Make-Believe*. Cambridge, MA: Harvard University Press.

Wang, Q. J., and C. Spence (2019) Drinking through rose-colored glasses: influence of wine colour on the perception of aroma and flavour in wine experts and novices. *Food Research International* 126: 108678.

Ward, J., B. Huckstep, and E. Tsakanikos (2006) Sound-colour synaesthesia: to what extent does it use cross-modal mechanisms common to us all? *Cortex* 42(2): 264–280.

Ward, J., and J. B. Mattingley (2006) Synaesthesia: an overview of contemporary findings and controversies. *Cortex* 42: 129–136. doi: 10.1016/S0010-9452(08)70336-8.

Watanabe, T., and T. Sato (1989) Effects of luminance contrast on color spreading and illusory contour in the neon color spreading effect. *Perception and Psychophysics* 45: 427–430.

Watkins, S., L. Shams, S. Tanaka, J. D. Haynes, and G. Rees (2006) Sound alters activity in human V1 in association with illusory visual perception. *NeuroImage* 31: 1247–1256.

Watzl, S. (2017) *Structuring Mind*. Oxford: Oxford University Press.

Weiskrantz, L. (2009) *Blindsight: A Case Study Spanning 35 Years and New Developments*. 2nd Edition. Oxford: Oxford University Press.

Winawer, J., N. Witthoft, M. C. Frank, L. Wu, A. R. Wade, and L. Boroditsky (2007) Russian blues reveal effects of language on color discrimination. *Proceedings of the National Academy of Sciences* 104(19): 7780–7785.

Wolfe, J. M. (1999) Inattentional amnesia. In: V. Coltheart (ed.), *Fleeting Memories. Cognition of Brief Visual Stimuli*. Cambidge: MIT Press, pp. 71–94.

Wollheim, R. (2003) What makes representational painting truly visual? *Aristotelian Society Supplementary Volume* 77(1): 131–147.

Woods, A. T., E. Poliakoff, D. M. Lloyd, J. Kuenzel, R. Hodson, H. Gonda, J. Batchelor, g. B. Dijksterhuis, and A. Thomas (2011) Effect of background noise on food perception. *Food Quality and Preference* 22: 42–47.

Yeshurun, Y., and M. Carrasco (1998) Attention improves or impairs visual performance by enhancing spatial resolution. *Nature* 396: 72–75.

Young, N. (2017) Hearing spaces. *Australasian Journal of Philosophy* 95: 242–255.

Young, B., and B. Nanay (2022a) Olfactory amodal completion. *Pacific Philosophical Quarterly* 103: 372–388.

Young, N., and B. Nanay (2022b) Audition and composite sensory individuals. In: A. Mroczko-Wasowicz, and R. Grush (eds.), *Sensory Individuals*. New York: Oxford University Press, pp. 179–192.

Zeman, A. Z. J., S. Della Sala, L. A. Torrens, V.-E. Gountouna, D. J. McGonigle, and R. H. Logie (2010) Loss of imagery phenomenology with intact visuo-spatial task performance: a case of 'blind imagination'. *Neuropsychologia* 48: 145–155.

Zeman, A., M. Dewar, and S. Della Sala (2015) Lives without imagery: congenital aphantasia. *Cortex* 73: 378–380.

INDEX

For Product Safety Concerns and Information please contact our EU
representative GPSR@taylorandfrancis.com
Taylor & Francis Verlag GmbH, Kaufingerstraße 24, 80331 München, Germany

www.ingramcontent.com/pod-product-compliance
Lightning Source LLC
Chambersburg PA
CBHW071746270326
41928CB00013B/2811